MORE
SECURE
LESS
FREE?

"Thank you Mark Sidel. This important book thoughtfully examines the interplay of antiterrorism policy and civil liberties in an unusually comprehensive and yet highly readable way. Especially valuable are the ways in which Sidel draws on his background in the worlds of law, philanthropy, and foreign affairs to depict the impact of antiterrorism measures at the state level, in our academic institutions, and among not-for-profits (including many of our most well-known foundations and charities). This is a book concerned Americans should read."

—William P. Alford, Henry L. Stimson Professor
of Law and Vice Dean, Harvard Law School

"Through a comprehensive analysis of America's antiterrorism policy, Sidel directly targets what Americans have lost in the 'war against terror.' *More Secure, Less Free?* is a mustread for anyone concerned about the increasing threats to liberty across the globe."

—Ravi Nair, Coordinator,
Asia Pacific Human Rights Network

"Mark Sidel takes us beyond the critique of the Patriot Act to examine what he rightly dubs the second wave of assaults on our civil liberties that has emerged since September 11. Detailing the rise and fall of TIPS, TIA, and CAPPS II, along with the continuing threats from the SEVIS and the MATRIX programs, the book reminds us that a broad-based campaign to oppose such programs can defeat the expansion of the government's authority to monitor and record the most sensitive and intimate details of the lives of innocent, law abiding Americans. Sidel also reminds us that the retreat of many of these 'second wave' programs does not preclude the emergence of a third or fourth wave of antiterrorism policies that can to bring us closer and closer to creating a true surveillance society."

—Barry Steinhardt, Director, Technology and
Liberty Program, American Civil Liberties Union

MORE SECURE LESS FREE?

Antiterrorism Policy
& Civil Liberties
after September 11

Mark Sidel

The University of Michigan Press
Ann Arbor

Copyright © by the University of Michigan 2004
All rights reserved
Published in the United States of America by
The University of Michigan Press
Manufactured in the United States of America
⊗ Printed on acid-free paper

2007   2006   2005   2004   4   3   2   1

A CIP catalog record for this book is available from the British Library.

Library of Congress Cataloging-in-Publication Data

Sidel, Mark.
More secure, less free? : antiterrorism policy
and civil liberties after September 11 / Mark Sidel.
p.   cm.
Includes bibliographical references and index.
ISBN 0-472-11428-x (cloth : alk. paper)
1. Terrorism— Prevention—Government policy—
United States.   2. Civil rights—United States.   I. Title.

HV6432.S547   2004
363.32'973—dc22

2004017532

To my parents & Kevin
& to Margaret, Rosie, & Thea

Contents

Acknowledgments

I am grateful to Jim Reische and Phil Pochoda for their commitment to the issues discussed in this volume. At the University of Iowa, the College of Law; the Obermann Center for Advanced Studies; and Eric Andersen, David Baldus, John Bergstrom, Amanda Bibb, Holly Carver, Corey Creekmur, Marcella David, Dana Denning, Carolyn Frisbie, Bill Hines, Linda Kerber, Chris Merrill, Lorna Olson, Jay Semel, and Karla Tonella provided support and assistance. For help or discussions on the themes discussed here, my thanks to Upala Banerjee, Barnett Baron, Warren Bass, William Flory, Richard Fries, Don Laughlin, Lawrence Liang, Mark Littlewood, Ravi Nair, Margaret Raymond, Carol Rose, Anthony Romero, Barry Steinhardt, Ben Stone, Shelton Stromquist, Jean Warburton, and Tung Yin, as well as three reviewers for the University of Michigan Press. From the Press, I am thankful for the work of Mary Bisbee-Beek, Felice Lau, Sarah Mann, Andrea Olson, Kevin Rennells, and Pete Sickman-Garner. For their tolerance while this volume was being written on a short deadline, I am particularly grateful to Margaret, Rosie, and Thea, as well as to the Palisa crew—Barnett Baron, Ifti Zaman, and Julie Wang. Several chapters took shape during a long weekend in northern Wisconsin; my thanks to Rosie, John Brogan, and the bankers of Kaukauna.

1

National Security, Civil Liberties, & Political Dissent in the United States
Background to the Current Crisis

This book is about the rippling and sometimes chilling effects of antiterrorism and national security policy and law on a range of aspects of American life since the terrorist attacks of September 11, 2001. The early outlines of this story are by now reasonably well known and have been discussed in detail by David Cole and James X. Dempsey, Nat Hentoff, Nancy Chang, Raneta Lawson Mack and Michael J. Kelly, and others—the early, quick passage of the USA Patriot Act and its influence in American life; the detention of citizens and noncitizens on suspicion or charges of terrorist activity; increasing government secrecy and regulation on such varied issues as bioterrorism, cybersecurity, and a host of other topics; and the growing resistance from civil libertarians, legislators, citizens, and many others.[1] This chapter surveys some of the key developments in that first stage of antiterrorism policy after September 11. It is but a brief summary of a wide and complex range of government measures and responses since September 11, intended to provide an overview for the general reader rather than in-depth scholarly analysis. Nor can this volume deal with a number of issues of international law, including the recent revelations of torture and abuse of prisoners in Iraq and Afghanistan.[2]

The core of this volume goes beyond earlier and more detailed studies of the Patriot Act, detentions and other early (and continuing) important issues. The chapters that follow analyze the effects of antiterrorism in American life by looking at five other important but more recent and generally under-studied aspects of antiterrorism beyond the Patriot Act. They seek to present these issues to a general audience concerned with policy issues.

- The struggle over some less well-understood recent "second wave" attempts to expand and extend federal antiterrorism policy, including the Total Information Awareness (TIA) data mining program supported by the Pentagon; the Justice Department's Operation TIPS (Terrorist Information and Prevention System) designed to create a system of national informants on suspicious individuals and occurrences; the CAPPS II (Computer Assisted Passenger Prescreening System II) air passenger monitoring and profiling program; Patriot Act II, the Justice Department's plans for a further strengthening of the Patriot Act, sometimes presumed dead but remaining alive, in part, through provisions in other legislation; the Defense Department's Eagle Eyes program of informants and reporting; and the Matrix (Multistate Anti-Terrorism Information Exchange) partnership of states and a private company undertaking data mining and profiling of millions of American citizens and residents.
- The development of antiterrorism strategies at the state level, including a first surge of strict new laws in the immediate wake of the September 11 attacks, followed by attempts to extend wiretapping and other authority, and the coalitions of resistance that have begun to spring up at the state level.
- The contradictory effects of antiterrorism policy on the

academic community, including government investigations and subpoenas, the chilling of academic and political discussion on some campuses, new restrictions on sensitive information, slowing and reductions in the issuance of visas to foreign students and scholars, and other limitations—within an American academic sector that, it must be said, remains extraordinarily free.

- The effects of antiterrorism in the American nonprofit sector, a topic until recently virtually ignored by American nonprofits and foundations, including the prosecutions of Muslim charitable leaders for alleged ties to terrorist organizations, the freezing of assets in those organizations, the chilling of giving to Muslim charities, and government attempts to provide guidelines for American nonprofits and foundations making grants overseas.
- A final chapter examines antiterrorism policy in three other countries—the United Kingdom, Australia, and India—as a lens to understand our own experience and to show that whereas some aspects of the debates over antiterrorism, security, and liberty are issues in more than one country, other facets of these conflicts are specific to particular societies.

Several themes begin to emerge here: the response to external threats is tightening through executive action and legislative acts at home; the means include enhanced surveillance of noncitizens in the United States (and some citizens as well), data gathering and profiling of American citizens and nonresident aliens alike, restrictions on use and release of official information, limitations on access of foreigners to American society, and a tightened environment for some aspects of the work of civil society and the nonprofit sector. These activities have taken place in several waves—an early wave of antiterrorist policy and law in the wake of the September 11 attacks that was questioned but largely enacted and then a second, overlap-

ping wave of antiterrorist government acts and legislative proposals that encountered much more substantial opposition and
an expanding coalition of critics.

Historical Roots of Government Control
Before September 11

All of this has roots in our history: episodes of resurgent government control and historical moments of the threat of
restriction on the exercise of our basic freedoms of speech and
assembly; discriminatory treatment against aliens and immigrants, particularly in times of national tragedy or difficulty;
increased surveillance of citizens and noncitizens; and persecu-
tion of political dissent.

One of the earliest such episodes occurred soon after the
founding of the American republic when, in the midst of fierce
conflict between warring parties, Congress adopted the Sedition Act of 1798. The Sedition Act criminalized political criticism of the new U.S. government and led to a number of convictions of political opponents of the Federalist Party, which
had sponsored the act. During the Civil War, President Lin-
coln sought to employ the military to maintain order in the
North and to end the right of citizens to challenge their detention through filing writs of habeas corpus. Under his orders the
Union army arrested thousands of nonmilitary citizen personnel, an action approved by Congress during the war. In 1866
the Supreme Court stepped in, reasserting the right to the writ
of habeas corpus and denying the role of the military to sup-
plant regular courts.[3] The Court ended with a ringing endorsement of the Constitution's role in protecting rights in a time of
national travail, a passage well worth reviewing now: "The
Constitution of the United States is a law for rulers and people,

equally in war and in peace, and covers with the shield of its protection all classes of men, at all times, and under all circumstances. No doctrine, involving more pernicious consequences, was ever invented by the wit of man than that any of its provisions can be suspended during any of the great exigencies of government."[4]

Controlling political dissent was again the goal of the Espionage Act of 1917, adopted in World War I during America's first period of sustained anticommunism. Under the Espionage Act, U.S. residents could be jailed for speaking, printing, writing, or publishing any "disloyal, profane, scurrilous, or abusive language" about the U.S. government or causing, inciting, or attempting to cause or incite "insubordination, disloyalty, mutiny, or refusal of duty" in the military.[5] The Espionage Act was upheld by the Supreme Court against a challenge that it violated the First Amendment rights of free speech and freedom of the press when political dissidents were charged with circulating leaflets "urg[ing] men to refuse to submit to the draft." The Court held that the doctrine of free speech "does not . . . protect a man from an injunction against uttering words that may have all the effect of force" and that such circumstances are justified "[w]hen a nation is at war [because] many things that might be said in times of peace are such a hindrance to its effort that their utterance will not be endured."[6] The Sedition Act of 1918 continued this treatment. Forced detentions were an issue once again in the midst of World War I, when anticommunism first entered American political and legal debate. Thousands of noncitizen residents of the United States were detained throughout the country in 1919 during the "Palmer Raids," which occurred after Attorney General A. Mitchell Palmer's home was attacked by anarchists. "Pains were taken to give spectacular publicity to the raids, and to make it appear that there was great and imminent public danger. . . . The arrested aliens were in most instances perfectly quiet and harmless working people."[7] More than five hundred were forced out of the country, "not one of whom was proved to pose a threat to the United States."[8]

Dissent was once again challenged in the Smith Act of 1940, which was adopted by Congress and signed into law by President Roosevelt at a time of growing conflict between the United States and the Soviet Union and the gradual growth of progressive and left wing groups and unions in the United States. Under the Smith Act, it became a crime to "knowingly or willfully advocate, abet, advise, or teach the duty, necessity, desirability, or propriety of overthrowing or destroying any government in the United States by force or violence" or "organiz[ing] . . . any . . . assembly of persons who teach, advocate, or encourage the overthrow or destruction of any government in the United States by force or violence."[9] The Smith Act was sparingly used, but it was employed in the late 1940s to convict eleven leaders of the U.S. Communist Party in a famous trial. That conviction was later upheld by the Supreme Court, rejecting a free speech challenge to the Smith Act and narrowing the free speech dissent available to political dissenters. Only in 1957 were the Smith Act convictions actually reversed by the Court.[10]

The most famous case of alien detention in American history is, of course, the Japanese internments of World War II. The details of this sorry episode are by now well known and have been covered in detail by Lawson Fusao Inada, Alfred Yen, Mark Tushnet, James Houston, Minoru Kiyota, and others. Over one hundred thousand American residents of Japanese origin, most of them U.S. citizens, were detained and interned in the western and southwestern United States beginning in 1942 under an executive order issued by President Roosevelt. In a time of international conflict and domestic emergency, a compliant Congress declined to challenge this blatant use of racial classifications to deny protection of the law to a particular racial group. And the Supreme Court upheld the executive branch's order against an appeal by a Japanese American, Fred Korematsu, who had been charged and convicted with resisting detention and internment. In dissent, Justice Murphy wrote prophetically: "Racial discrimination in any form and in any degree has no justifiable part whatever in our democratic way of life. . . . [American residents of Japanese origin and other racial groups] must . . . be treated at all times as the heirs of the American experiment and as entitled to all the rights and freedoms guaranteed by the Constitution."[11] About forty years later, Korematsu's conviction was set aside by a federal judge in California, with the government's consent, and Congress—much belatedly—sought to undo its earlier compliance by adopting an act recognizing that the internments had been wrong, providing an apology and a small financial sum.[12]

The Cold War and McCarthy periods stand as perhaps the most widespread use of law to suppress disagreement and punish dissenting citizens and noncitizens in recent American history. The history of this period, too, is well known. In the McCarthy era, a member of Congress and a congressional committee, the House Un-American Affairs Committee, took the lead in repressive tactics. Not that the executive branch was passive: some of the key mechanisms of the Cold War and the McCarthy era—such as federal investigations, loyalty oaths, surveillance, and other tactics—depended heavily on surging executive power. The Supreme Court did not begin to reassert its role until 1957, and it was not until 1967, in *U.S. v. Robel*, that the Court unambiguously reasserted freedom of association when Chief Justice Earl Warren noted: "It would indeed be ironic if, in the name of national defense, we would sanction the subversion of one of those liberties—the freedom of association—which makes the defense of the Nation worth-while."[13]

Attempts to silence dissent were, of course, prominent features of executive branch strategies during the Vietnam War era. As in the Cold War and McCarthy eras, the Federal Bureau of Investigation was a key tool of executive branch interference with free speech and free association to oppose progressive and radical groups—and eventually to oppose the wide swath of American society that came to protest U.S. involvement in the war in Vietnam. These government activities took a number of forms, but among the most well known was an FBI-wide counterintelligence and antiactivist program known as COINTELPRO. The program went far beyond research or the building of intelligence files—it was intended to "expose, disrupt, misdirect, discredit, or otherwise neutralize" civil rights, women's, trade union, and antiwar organizations and individuals affiliated with them, beginning in the mid-1950s and extending until the early 1970s.

Congress roused itself to the threats from the FBI and COINTELPRO only twenty years after the program was established, in 1976, when a Senate committee headed by Senator Frank Church revealed the full extent of the program and severely criticized it. The ramifications of COINTELPRO continue to this day. In the wake of the Church hearings, FBI rules limiting domestic security investigations were issued in 1976, then relaxed in 1983 under President Reagan and again in 2002 under President Bush.[14]

Antiterrorism Policy & Law after September 11
The First Wave

The most well known of the post–September 11 antiterrorism tools, and the first major one enacted, is the law referred to as the USA Patriot Act—an abbreviation for the full title of Public Law 107-56, which was signed into law by President Bush on October 26, 2001: "The Uniting and Strengthening America by Providing Appropriate Tools Required to Intercept and Obstruct Terrorism Act." The rapid adoption of antiterrorism measures—often without sufficient congressional review—actually began within days of the September 11 tragedy. As early as September 13, 2001, Senator Orrin Hatch proposed loosening the restrictions on wiretapping of phones and other communications. Senator Patrick Leahy of Vermont tried to slow the progress of this legislation: "I worry that we may run into the situation where—all of us have joined together in our horror at these despicable, murderous acts in New York and at the Pentagon—we do not want to change our laws so that it comes back to bite us later on."[15] But those amendments passed quickly, and there was more to come.

As Senator Leahy put it:

What does this do to help the men and women in New York and their families and those children who were orphans in an instant, a horrible instant? . . . Maybe the Senate wants to just go ahead and adopt new abilities to wiretap our citizens. Maybe they want to adopt new abilities to go into people's computers. Maybe that will make us feel safer. Maybe. And maybe what the terrorists have done made us a little bit less safe. Maybe they have increased Big Brother in this country. . . . [D]o we really show respect to the American people by slapping something together, something that nobody on the floor can explain, and say we are changing the duties of the Attorney General, the Director of the CIA, the U.S. attorneys, we are going to change your rights as Americans, your rights to privacy? We are going to do it with no hearings, no debate. . . . If we are going to change habeas corpus, change our rights as Americans, if we are going to change search and seizure provisions, if we are going to give new rights for State investigators to come into Federal court to seek remedies in the already overcrowded Federal courts, fine, the Senate can do that. But what have we done to stop terrorism and to help the people in New York and the survivors at the Pentagon?[16]

In the words of Attorney General John Ashcroft, the act "provide[s] the security that ensures liberty. . . . First, it closes the gaping holes in our ability to investigate terrorists. Second, the Patriot Act updates our anti-terrorism laws to meet the challenges of new technology, and new threats. Third, the Patriot Act has allowed us to build an extensive team that shares information and fights terrorism together."[17] Civil libertarians saw it differently. In the words of the American Civil Liberties Union (ACLU), the act was "an overnight revision of the nation's surveillance laws that vastly expanded the government's authority to spy on its own citizens, while simultaneously reducing checks and balances on those powers such as judicial oversight, public accountability, and the ability to challenge government searches in court."[18]

The Patriot Act is a complex and broad statute, and this brief review for the general reader seeks only to provide a general picture of the act. The Patriot Act has been covered in considerable detail by a number of legal and other scholarly commentators; that in-depth legal and scholarly analysis of the Patriot Act is cited in the Further Readings section as well as in the endnotes. The Patriot Act provided the executive branch with an expanded menu of authority to act against various forms of crime and terrorism, very broadly defined. Little here was actually new, at least in the form of legislative proposals, and many of those proposals were originally responses not to terrorism but to the use of rapidly expanding new technologies such as cell phones and e-mail. But the political environment after September 11 provided the opportunity for congressional adoption, and, as other commentators have discussed, the debate was over rapidly.[19] Though adopted in less than two months, the Patriot Act is a lengthy and highly complex statute. In this chapter, we discuss in very general terms some of its most important or controversial elements before moving on to a discussion in more detail of the second wave of antiterrorist policy and law in chapter 2.

The New Crime of Domestic Terrorism

The Patriot Act enlarged the laws countering terrorism to provide for a new crime of "domestic terrorism," under which a range of law enforcement agencies could conduct investigations, surveillance, wiretapping, and other actions against organizations and individuals in the United States. The new offense was defined broadly to include "acts dangerous to human life" intended to "influence the policy of the government by intimidation or coercion." And even providing assistance to such a group—without any involvement in direct "terrorist" activities—may trigger prosecution under the act. The breadth of this definition of domestic terrorism has been the subject of substantial controversy. Civil libertarians, conservative privacy activists, and others cite a range of organizations—including the antiabortion group Operation Rescue—as examples of groups that could come within the new definition of domestic terrorism, and they argue that investigation and prosecution of terrorists are already amply covered under existing criminal law. Others argue that these concerns are substantially overdrawn, that the new powers will be sparsely employed, and that sufficient checks are in place to limit government excesses. It is worth noting that noncitizens may be at particular risk under the new crime of "domestic terrorism," for noncitizen aliens resident in the United States may be held or deported if such an individual merely donates to or is a member of a group that is considered a terrorist organization.

The New Surveillance & Search Powers of Law Enforcement

The Problem of "Secret Searches"   Under section 213 of the act, law enforcement organizations are permitted to undertake secret searches, often called "sneak and peek" searches, without informing the subjects of those searches, allowing wider surveillance than permissible before to the FBI and other law enforcement authorities. The Justice Department has not denied that such searches have occurred, though it refuses to provide detailed data on the use of the section 213 power. And the act does not limit this power to terrorism investigations— it is now available for non-terror-related criminal investigations as well.

New Dangers to Personal Records   The Patriot Act also permits law enforcement authorities to obtain medical, financial, student, computer, and other personal records from "third party" holders of those records under section 215, without notice to the target of the investigation, without explicitly tying the search to terrorism or spying, by recourse to the semisecret Foreign Intelligence Surveillance Court. Section 215 was drafted broadly enough to allow the FBI to require public libraries, university libraries, bookstores, medical offices, doctors, Internet service providers, and other record holders to provide information. For example, libraries and bookstores can be required to supply data about individuals' reading habits, which has sparked significant public outcry and an alliance between traditional civil liberties groups and the library, bookselling, and publishing communities. Law enforcement authorities may now obtain information without showing a reasonable suspicion of criminal activity or "probable cause" under the Fourth Amendment to the Constitution. So even speech activities, such as political statements or materials read can trigger this sort of largely unrestricted surveillance and information order. Nor is the government required to show that the person concerned is an "agent of a foreign power," as previously required by law.

The American Civil Liberties Union and other civil libertarians assert that section 215 of the Patriot Act violates First Amendment protections of free speech (for those subject to record production orders and for those whose searches have been triggered by the exercise of free speech), Fourth Amendment protections against government searches without probable cause, and Fourth and Fifth Amendment protections of due process.

Section 505 of the act also permits federal authorities to obtain records from credit reporting firms, Internet service providers, and telecommunications companies through "National Security Letters" issued by the FBI without a requirement of suspicion that the individual targeted is involved in terrorism. The recipients of law enforcement orders under either section 215 or section 505 are generally prohibited from disclosing the order to the target, the press, activists, or anyone other than those required to know in order to facilitate the provision of the information to the authorities.

As discussed later in this chapter, faced with substantial opposition from a growing alliance of libraries and other information providers and archivists, the government was forced to announce in the fall of 2003 that section 215 had not yet been specifically employed to obtain information from libraries or other sources. In 2003 and 2004 a national movement to amend section 215 of the Patriot Act gathered force, with a coalition of civil liberties organizations, the American Booksellers Association, American Library Association, Gun Owners of America, the American Conservative Union, and other conservative groups, along with more than a million petition signers lobbying for the SAFE Act, which would relax some of section 215 and other more severe portions of the Patriot Act.

At the same time, new doubts arose about the use of section 215 after the attorney general's 2003 statement that it had not yet been employed. In May 2004, the Justice Department told a Detroit federal district court judge hearing an ACLU challenge to section 215 that the Justice Department could not "undertake an obligation to keep the court informed on an ongoing basis if and when the government seeks a section 215 order," raising the possibility that section 215 might have been utilized since the attorney general's 2003 statement.[20] No such assurances were made with respect to section 505, and in fact a significant number of National Security Letters seem to have been issued.[21]

Wiretapping and Foreign Intelligence   Earlier law had maintained a certain barrier between the gathering of information for intelligence purposes and for criminal investigation purposes. As the Lawyers Committee for Human Rights puts it: "law enforcement could not use the intelligence division to collect information for a criminal case which it would otherwise be barred from collecting due to insufficient evidence to support a search warrant within the criminal justice system."[22] The Patriot Act has substantially lowered this wall, providing the government with enhanced powers to collect information related to foreign intelligence and loosening the requirements for that collection of information. Under the act, the Justice Department has reduced the barrier between intelligence surveillance and criminal investigations, increasing the information available to prosecutors on non-intelligence-related crimes by allowing them access to data collected during intelligence wiretaps and surveillance. Now only a "significant" purpose of the search need be collecting foreign intelligence, a considerably less restricted standard than existed under the Foreign Intelligence Surveillance Act of 1978 (FISA). The ease with which wiretapping orders may now be obtained under FISA, after the relaxing amendments of the Patriot Act; the easy availability of "emergency" FISA orders—with even fewer protections; and the weakening of the wall between intelligence investigations and criminal prosecutions may have contributed to the fact that "FISA orders now account for just over half of all federal wiretapping conducted" according to a major human rights organization.[23]

Dealing with Technology and Terrorism: The Addresses and Content of Communications   The Patriot Act also expands the use of so-called trap and trace searches, permitting the government to gather information based on the "addresses" of communications rather than the content of those communications. This procedure has been allowed in a limited form for a number of years, but section 214 expands the ability of the government to undertake the trap and trace (also called "pen register") searches by enlarging such wiretapping orders issued by a federal judge to cover the entire country, not just the specific judicial district in which they are issued; allowing agents to complete required information after a judicial order has been issued; and applying the trap and trace rationale to the Internet. Each of these powers potentially substantially weakens earlier protections.

The CIA, the FBI, and Domestic Surveillance   In the wake of the abuses of the 1950s, 1960s, and 1970s, the Central Intelligence Agency had been prohibited from engaging in domestic intelligence work, and the FBI had been prohibited from conducting surveillance on political dissidents outside normal investigative limits. The Patriot Act now provides the CIA, through the director of central intelligence, with a role in defining domestic intelligence requirements. And in May 2002, the attorney general sharply expanded the ability of the FBI to monitor political organizations and public dissent, reversing earlier regulations adopted after the abuses of the 1960s and 1970s.[24]

Other surveillance mechanisms, operating or failed—such as the Total Information Awareness project established at the Defense Department, Operation TIPS, watch lists maintained over air travel by the Transportation Security Administration, plans for the passenger monitoring and profiling system, CAPPS II, including the uses of CAPPS II beyond identifying potential terrorists, the Matrix database in development at the state level, and the military's Eagle Eyes program, are discussed in chapter 2.

The Treatment of Noncitizens

Under the Patriot Act, residents of the United States who are not American citizens came under special scrutiny. In the immediate wake of the September 11 attacks, immigration and interrogation sweeps were undertaken against thousands of immigrants and aliens, many of Arab and Muslim background. Well over a thousand were detained in 2001 and 2002, for an average of eighty days each, in a process that the Justice Department's own inspector general later called "indiscriminate and haphazard." Those detentions were also plagued by extensions of time in custody without charge at the order of the Justice Department, refusals to allow communications with lawyers, and a policy of refusing bond to those picked up in the initial sweeps. A host of public interest legal organizations filed a suit in 2001 seeking the names and circumstances of those picked up in the post–September 11 sweeps. After an initial victory, a federal appellate court allowed the government to retain secrecy over the sweeps, on the grounds that the "judiciary owes some measure of deference to the executive in cases implicating national security."[25]

Between the summer of 2002 and late April 2003, the Justice Department conducted a much-criticized "registration" program for noncitizens from some 25 countries, mostly Arab and Muslim states. This National Security Exit-Entry Registration System (NSEERS) required males from 16 to 45 years old to appear at Immigration and Naturalization Service offices for fingerprinting, pictures, and questioning. More than 1,800 were detained after seeking to comply with the registration rules, and the treatment of those detained was often odious. According to Human Rights First, "[I]n Los Angeles, for example, about 400 men and boys were detained during the first phase of call-in registration. Some were handcuffed and had their legs put in shackles; others were hosed down with cold water or forced to sleep standing up because of overcrowding."[26] Civil liberties and mainstream organizations criticized the haphazard nature of the registration program, some organizations likened it to singling out Jews during the Nazi era, and conservatives called the program ineffective and overreaching.[27] A number of aliens were deported or barred from returning to the United States, and none have, it appears, been charged with any terrorist activity as a result of the registration program as of early 2004.

Interviews were also conducted with several thousand Arab and Muslim men in 2002 and 2003, a process extended to Iraqi-born citizens and aliens when war with Iraq was imminent. Asylum seekers from thirty-three suspect Arab and Muslim nations were also automatically detained in a program called "Operation Liberty Shield." And of perhaps even more concern for the future, the number of refugees invited to settle in the United States has been on a substantial decline since September 11, and local police and other authorities are increasingly being drawn into federal immigration enforcement.

The Struggle over the Detainees

Attempts to understand the legal and policy implications of the controversial detentions since the September 11 attacks are complicated by the fact that the detainees held by the U.S. government fall into not one but several categories.[28]

Noncitizen Combatant Detainees Held at Guantanamo Bay   One important category of post–September 11 detainees is noncitizen, international detainees taken into custody in Afghanistan, Pakistan, Bosnia, and elsewhere. By 2003, over six hundred of those "battlefield detainees" from more than forty countries were held at Guantanamo Bay at a camp established at a U.S. naval facility. The Guantanamo detainees have not been identified as "combatants" by the U.S. government, for that would require, in most cases, that the United States comply with the Geneva conventions requirements for protection of prisoners of war. Nor have the Guantanamo detainees been identified as criminal suspects, for that would entitle them to certain rights in the U.S. criminal justice system. The holding of detainees with British and Australian citizenship has prompted diplomatic tension with those countries. Legal challenges by detainees' families to the detentions have also failed, initially because the detainees were being held at Cuba-leased Guantanamo Bay, an area that the courts defined as under U.S. "jurisdiction and control" rather than "sovereign" U.S. territory subject to judicial mandate.

The distinction between "prisoner of war," entitled to certain internationally mandated protections, and "enemy combatant" or "battlefield detainee," entitled to far fewer legal protections, has been a particularly difficult issue. Noncitizens accused of international terrorism or violations of the law of war who are not prisoners of war may eventually be tried under the controversial military commissions established by the U.S. government in the fall of 2002. The commissions, not yet operating, would provide some but not all of the procedural guarantees of a regular court, with substantial constraints on legal representation. The proceedings may also be closed to the public. The threat of trying international detainees in U.S. military commissions has sparked considerable opposition among key U.S. allies and others around the world, as well as in the United States, with legal scholars and diplomats arguing that trial in regular courts or extradition home to face trial in home countries are the only legal alternatives available to the United States. In late 2003 the U.S. Supreme Court agreed to hear arguments on the Guantanamo detentions, setting the stage for a judicial resolution of the detainees' status, the use of indefinite detention, and perhaps the circumstances of potential trials.

The Knotty Problem of Citizen Combatants Captured Abroad or Arrested in the United States   In addition to the noncitizens held at Guantanamo, several U.S. citizens have been held, and in one case charged and convicted, for terrorism-related offenses. Treatment has varied depending on the circumstances of these individuals' capture or arrest, their activities abroad, the evidence available against them, and other variables with which we may not be entirely familiar. The American John Walker Lindh was captured with the Taliban in Afghanistan, held by U.S. forces under harsh circumstances, and questioned by the FBI after the FBI had notice that Lindh's family had hired a lawyer for him. Lindh was then imprisoned in the United States and then, through the criminal justice system, pled guilty to assisting the Taliban.

James Ujaama is a second and considerably less well-known U.S. citizen held by the United States for terrorism- and war-related offenses. Ujaama was arrested in the United States in the summer of 2002 and charged with conspiracy to provide support to Al Qaeda through plans to establish a terrorist training camp in Oregon. His case was handled through the regular criminal justice system. Ujaama pled guilty in 2003, and he was sentenced to two years in prison.

The cases of two other U.S. citizens held by the U.S. government have turned out to be far more complex. One of these citizens, Yaser Hamdi, was captured abroad, in Afghanistan. Another, Jose Padilla, was arrested in Chicago. Both have been held as enemy combatants and refused counsel, and their cases have become major tests of government policy toward citizen detainees.

Yaser Hamdi was born in Baton Rouge and spent most of his childhood in Saudi Arabia. Like Lindh, he was captured in Afghanistan, allegedly while assisting the Taliban—but because he is being held incommunicado and the government has released little information about him, we know equally little about his alleged activities. After his capture in Afghanistan in 2001, Hamdi was taken to Guantanamo and then transferred to a military prison in Charleston, South Carolina, after his U.S. citizenship was confirmed.

Hamdi was named an enemy combatant by the government and denied access to a lawyer, but he has not been charged. In 2002 a U.S. federal judge ordered that Hamdi be able to meet with a public defender. When an appellate court vacated that order the district judge questioned the government's designation of Hamdi as an enemy combatant in more forceful terms, ordering production of documents to substantiate that designation. The appellate court again vacated the district judge's order, holding that "Hamdi's detention conforms with a legitimate exercise of the war powers given the executive." But it also refused to accept the notion that "with no meaningful judicial review, any American citizen alleged to be an enemy combatant could be detained indefinitely without charges or counsel on the government's say-so." And there were several ringing dissents. In late 2003, the government finally allowed Hamdi access to a lawyer. And in early 2004, the Supreme Court agreed to hear the Hamdi case and to decide whether U.S. citizens such as Hamdi, detained outside the United States, may be held indefinitely and under what conditions.[29]

Jose Padilla is another U.S. citizen, now held outside the criminal justice system, whose case has produced significant controversy. Padilla was arrested at O'Hare Airport in Chicago in 2002 and designated an enemy combatant. The attorney general has called him a "known terrorist" who intended to set off a radioactive "dirty bomb" on U.S. territory. Padilla is being held with Hamdi at a naval base in South Carolina and, like Hamdi, was denied access to a lawyer for many months. In Padilla's case, a federal appellate court in New York decided that the government's mere assertion that Padilla was an enemy combatant was insufficient to allow him to be held indefinitely, basing its decision in part on Padilla's capture within the United States rather than in a foreign country. The Justice Department immediately sought review of that decision in the Supreme Court, and the Supreme Court agreed to hear the Padilla case in spring 2004.

Thus the stage was set for the U.S. Supreme Court to hear and decide on the lawfulness of the government's detention of over six hundred noncitizens on Guantanamo, as well as the detention of a U.S. citizen captured overseas (Hamdi) and a U.S. citizen arrested in the United States (Padilla) on terrorism and national security offenses. At issue are two crucial and linked concerns—the possibly varying rights of detainees of these various kinds (foreigners, citizens captured abroad, and citizens arrested in the United States) and also the authority of the courts to review determinations made by the federal government in its war powers and national security roles.

The Remaining Detainees: Noncitizens Arrested in the United States   Two other detainee cases have raised special controversy. Ali Saleh Kahlah al-Marri, a citizen of Qatar, was arrested in the United States at the end of 2001 on suspicion of assisting Al Qaeda. Rather than initially being held as an enemy combatant, al-Marri was processed through the criminal justice system and charged with a variety of terrorism-related financial and other crimes. But shortly before his trial was to begin, the government changed Hamdi's status to enemy combatant, dismissed the charges against him, and transferred him to the same Charleston military jail holding Hamdi and Padilla. There he is not allowed access to the lawyers who were defending him on the criminal charges.

It is not clear why the U.S. government made this abrupt choice. Some civil liberties organizations believe that al-Marri had a reasonable chance of suppressing some of the government's evidence in the criminal case and perhaps even of winning acquittal. The government has said that new information was developed on al-Marri's ties to terrorism and that it was "confident" that the Justice Department would have won the criminal case.[30]

A considerably more well-known noncitizen detainee arrested in the United States has also been threatened with a change in status from criminal defendant—with a range of protections available—to enemy combatant, particularly if the government does not have its way with the conduct of his trial. This is Zacarias Moussaoui, an Arab who grew up in France,[31] who was charged with assisting the September 11 terrorists. For nearly a year and a half, Moussaoui was allowed to represent himself, and his erratic filings and statements further disrupted the proceedings in his case. But in 2003, a federal district court decided that Moussaoui had the right to take a deposition from an alleged Al Qaeda member captured in Pakistan. The government appealed, arguing that upholding the deposition order would interfere with military operations and interrogations abroad and that the individual captured in Pakistan was outside the authority of the federal courts.

In the summer of 2003, the government formally refused to allow Moussaoui to question the alleged Al Qaeda member held in Pakistan and implicitly threatened to transfer Moussaoui to incommunicado, enemy combatant status if it lost that battle.[32] In response, the federal court dismissed most of the charges against Moussaoui and refused to allow consideration of the death penalty because Moussaoui could not gather evidence to support his case. The government appealed to a federal appellate court, where the matter remained in early 2004.[33]

In June 2004, the U.S. Supreme Court ruled that both U.S. citizens and noncitizens held in the wake of September 11 may have access to the American courts to challenge their detention and treatment. In the *Hamdi* case, the Court ruled that the president had the authority to detain Hamdi and other U.S. citizens as alleged enemy combatants—but the Court refused to deny Hamdi and other U.S. citizen detainees access to the courts to challenge such detentions and their treatment. In a separate case, *Rasul v. Bush*, the nearly 600 noncitizens held at Guantanamo Bay were also permitted to challenge their detention in the courts. In the case of Jose Padilla, the Court, by a 5-4 decision, required that Padilla refile his case in a lower federal court, thereby avoiding a direct decision on that matter. "Striking the proper constitutional balance here is of great importance to the Nation during this period of ongoing combat," wrote Justice Sandra Day O'Connor in the *Hamdi* decision. "But it is equally vital that our calculus not give short shrift to the values that this country holds dear or to the privilege that is American citizenship. It is during our most challenging and uncertain moments that our Nation's commitment to due process is most severely tested; and it is in those times that we must preserve our commitment at home to the principles for which we fight abroad. ... [A] state of war is not a blank check for the President when it comes to the rights of the Nation's citizens."[34]

The New Attacks on Releasing Government Information

Because of a range of actions separate from the Patriot Act, public access to official information has clearly suffered since September 11. In the first wave of executive action after the attacks, the Justice Department limited citizens' access to government information under the Freedom of Information Act by increasing the use of exemptions to providing information. The department also announced that it would defend agencies that decline to release information if that refusal had a "sound legal basis." This substantially weakened an earlier standard for release of official information under the act—that information should be released unless it would result in "foreseeable harm." Now a government agency need not argue or show foreseeable harm but only demonstrate that it has a sound legal basis under the act to refuse to give up information. Under the 2002 Homeland Security Act, Congress also added a broad and vaguely worded exemption for information on "security or critical infrastructure" to the range of data that the government need not disclose. Furthermore, as discussed in chapter 4, the White House has also strongly pushed government agencies to refuse to release a broad category of "sensitive but non-classified material," a stance reinforced in the Homeland Security Act, leading to substantial controversy in the academic world, and the president has issued an executive order strengthening the classification process and erecting stronger barriers to declassification of official information.

The executive branch's reluctance to release information extends beyond the public to Congress, which has had immense difficulties in obtaining information on the implementation of the Patriot Act; the numbers and status of detainees; the activities of the Foreign Intelligence Surveillance Court; and plans for new legislation, including the Patriot Act II discussed in chapter 2. For the most part, the courts have upheld the government's considerably broader reading of the Freedom of Information Act since late 2001, part of an initial pattern of deference to the executive branch that was among the troubling aspects of the post–September 11 era. One interesting exception was the decision by the U.S. Court of Appeals for the Sixth Circuit in the case involving Rabih Haddad, the Ann Arbor Muslim leader who was also among the leaders of the Global Relief Foundation, discussed in chapter 4. There an appellate court held that the government could not entirely close deportation hearings to the press under the First Amendment.

The Patriot Act & the Growing Power of Alliance

The Justice Department has consistently refused to provide any detailed information on the use of the Patriot Act, either to the public or to Congress, including information on the actual uses of the new surveillance powers provided to law enforcement under the act. This is disturbing because it indicates a lack of executive branch accountability to Congress. But in another sense the increasing willingness of Congress—often spurred by constituents' rage—to ask about the uses of the Patriot Act in practice may also bode well for the reawakening of a somewhat compliant legislature.

In the face of growing criticism from librarians, library associations, publishing and bookselling associations, and other groups—and a growing alliance between those organizations and civil liberties forces—the Justice Department gave way a bit in an attempt to defuse the controversy over a particularly problematic part of the act: section 215. As mentioned previously, section 215 allows for tracking of bookstore and library use and seizure of organizational files, computers, and other materials but also prohibits those ordered to provide information—such as bookstores and libraries—from divulging those requests. The attorney general announced in October 2003 that the government has not yet made use of section 215 in its investigatory work. The notification, which came in the form of declassification of the secret information relating to the use of section 215, was for the purpose "that the public not be misled regarding the manner in which the U.S. Department of Justice, and the FBI in particular, have been utilizing the authorities provided in the . . . Act." The attorney general pointedly noted that the Justice Department and the FBI "have not been able to counter the troubling amount of public distortion and misinformation in connection with Section 215."[35]

The politics of this begrudging admission were perhaps more important than its legal implications, for the statement clearly showed the power of civil liberties and pro-privacy groups in alliance with powerful social, cultural, and economic actors such as public libraries, university libraries, and the bookselling industry. In legal terms it probably meant somewhat less, for the government has certain other tools available (such as National Security Letters) to obtain similar information. And, as one prominent Washington watchdog organization, OMB (Office of Management and Budget) Watch, noted: "The fact that Section 215 has never been invoked may give some small comfort to those who fear the Patriot Act gives government unchecked and out-of-balance powers. In the end, such questions—and the underlying public distrust of government—can be put to rest only when government is less secretive, reports forthrightly on its use of the tools our laws grant it, and thereby shows a stronger commitment to the democratic process."[36] As noted earlier, the Justice Department's refusal to provide information on section 215 usage to a federal court in Detroit hearing a civil liberties challenge to the provision raised some renewed concerns in 2004 about the utilization of section 215 after the attorney general's September 2003 assertion that it had not yet been used.

This is but one example of the power of alliance to force retreats by the government in the implementation of antiterrorist law and policy. It is important not to overstate the importance of those retreats. But it also is important to note, as the following chapters often do, that growing alliances—often involving civil libertarians; conservative privacy activists; libertarians; and even gun owners, antiabortion activists, and others—have played substantial roles in defeating or slowing the enactment or implementation of antiterrorist measures, especially in the second wave of measures proposed after the Patriot Act. As discussed in chapter 2, the American Civil Liberties Union has played a leading role in forming these alliances.

Considerable portions of the more controversial parts of the original Patriot Act—particularly those relating to surveillance authority and foreign intelligence—will "sunset," or expire, at the end of 2005 as the result of compromises made when the Patriot Act was originally adopted in 2001. These sunset provisions include wiretapping in terrorism cases, sharing of wiretaps and foreign intelligence information, roving wiretaps, "trap and trace" authority, the controversial access to business records (the "library" issues), national service of search warrants, and other important provisions.[37] Already the battle has been joined on whether these important parts of the Patriot Act should be renewed—as the president forcefully advocated in his State of the Union speech in January 2004— or scrapped. The alliance building of the last several years on particular portions of the act, and particularly on second wave initiatives after that—such as TIA, Patriot Act II, TIPS, and other efforts mentioned earlier and discussed in detail in chapter 2—will no doubt play a critical role in the results of this debate when the Patriot Act comes up for reconsideration in Congress, at least in some form, in 2004 or 2005.

In the building of opposition alliances and the approaching sunset clauses, the Patriot Act adopted with such fervor and speed after the 2001 attacks may now be coming full circle. Some elements of the conservative and libertarian community have already sided with civil libertarians and others against the act or particular portions of it. Even Viet Dinh, the former high ranking Justice Department official who, as head of the Office of Legal Counsel, played a substantial role in drafting the Patriot Act, Patriot Act II, and other measures, said in early 2004 that "there has . . . to be some sort of access to counsel and some sort of process" for detained U.S. citizens like Jose Padilla.[38] The Patriot Act went far, though perhaps not as far as its critics have charged, and it continues to hold substantial potential danger in the powers it gives government—even if government is not actually using those powers yet. But the Patriot Act was also accompanied by strong state activities to expand antiterrorist wiretap and surveillance authority, and it would soon be followed by a second wave of antiterrorist policies and government programs. Opposition also strengthened, often in an innovative alliance between traditional civil liberties advocates, conservatives, libertarians concerned with privacy and government power, and a range of other constituencies. And antiterrorism policies and program came to have increasing effects on the academic and nonprofit sectors. We now turn to these developments.

2

The Second Wave of Antiterrorism Law & Policy

Antiterrorism policy since September 11 has often been equated with the Patriot Act. But it is much more. The years 2002, 2003, and early 2004 saw the launching of an overlapping second wave of programs aimed against terrorism, efforts that are crucially important for understanding the shape of antiterrorism policy in the United States after the 2001 attacks. But the second wave is also important because these new efforts galvanized opposition, across a wide political spectrum, that surpassed what was feasible in the few short weeks before the Patriot Act was passed in the immediate wake of September 11. These programs and proposals represent not only the next steps in the government's plans for increased monitoring, surveillance, and prosecution but also a substantial advance in the strategies and tactics of resistance. And, until the battle over reauthorization or amendment of the Patriot Act is finally joined in earnest, it is these initiatives that may well be the fulcrum of conflict over antiterrorism policy.

A Law Lying in Wait The Patriot Act II

If there were ever a law lying in wait for another tragic terrorist attack, it is the draft legislation that the press and critics have called "Patriot Act II." Virtually since the moment the Patriot Act was enacted, there had been rumors that the Justice Department wanted more powers available to use against suspected terrorists and their supporters in the United States and that the attorney general and the White House would press quickly for more authority in the event of another significant terrorist event, if not before. From the government's perspective, such preparatory work could seem only prudent, given the risks that faced the United States. But the Justice Department consistently denied that a second, even more severe, Patriot Act had been drafted, while occasionally acknowledging that various new "proposals," "tools," or "ideas" were under consideration.

In early February 2003, the Washington-based Center for Public Integrity obtained and published an extraordinary document—the January 2003 draft of a bill called the "Domestic Security Enhancement Act of 2003."[1] Drafted (or at least distributed) by the Office of Legal Policy in the Justice Department, the act—quickly dubbed "Patriot Act II" by critics and the press alike—would tighten some of the provisions of the Patriot Act that had been weakened by Congress in late 2001, while adding new provisions. This new Patriot Act would, if enacted, significantly expand government power to spy on citizens; allow sharing of personal data among federal, state, and local governments; further reduce the curbs imposed on police spying after abuses in the 1960s and 1970s; increase government secrecy in environmental, immigration, and other important areas; encourage informing on fellow citizens by shielding informers; and further criminalize political activities that the government might allege are related to terrorism.

If Americans doubted that it was possible in American democracy to expand federal powers and harden federal action much beyond the Patriot Act, their misunderstandings might be cleared up quickly by the Domestic Security Enhancement Act. If passed, the act would bar Justice Department disclosure of information about alleged terrorism-related detainees; virtually eliminate public access to industry "worst case scenario" documents prepared for the Environmental Protection Agency; create a "suspected terrorist" DNA database that could include citizens as well as noncitizens and allow government inclusion of people merely suspected of "association" with "suspected" terrorists; codify the presumption of pretrial detention for citizens or noncitizens suspected of terrorist activity; and allow the U.S. government to "expatriate"—take away the citizenship of—citizens associated with terrorist groups, an association that might be so broadly defined as to include participating in legal activities of a designated terrorist group, such as demonstrations.

The Patriot Act II would also allow secret detention of citizens and noncitizens suspected of terrorism for up to fifteen days without informing courts or lawyers; permit wiretapping of citizens and noncitizens for fifteen days entirely on the authority of the attorney general and without requiring court approval; terminate court-approved or court-mandated restrictions on police surveillance and spying on political activists that date from the abuses committed by the FBI and local police departments in the 1960s; and impose the death penalty for a range of protests that "involve violent acts or acts dangerous to human life," a broad definition that might encompass, for example, Greenpeace operations if a death resulted from such protest.

The act goes still further—almost, at times, seeming to be a laundry list of the lobbying requests of what might be called the "hard state" forces. Federal agents would not be subject to prosecution for engaging in illegal wiretapping or surveillance if they had been following the instructions of senior government officials. The act would prevent defense lawyers from opposing the use of secret evidence in criminal proceedings involving terrorism. It would allow the federal government to share personal data about American citizens with state and local authorities without any alleged or proven connection to terrorism. It would provide immunity for phoning in unsupported, even reckless, "terrorism tips" to law enforcement authorities. The act would enable the attorney general to summarily deport—without lawyers or hearings—noncitizens, including lawful, often long-term, permanent residents, if the attorney general merely labels them a threat to national security.

The act would also significantly cut into the habeas corpus protections that have shielded Americans and lawful permanent residents from government detention since the adoption of the U.S. Constitution. Under the act, legal permanent residents convicted of minor crimes would not be accorded hearings and would be removable from the country, and the act would significantly hamper courts from exercising habeas corpus review of those administrative decisions. The act would enable the government to expatriate any citizen who "provid[es] material support . . . to . . . a terrorist group designated" by the federal government if the organization is "engaged in hostilities" with the United States or its "national security interests."[2]

By itself, this provision does not seem particularly drastic. But recall that the original Patriot Act substantially broadened the range of organizations that could be designated as "terrorist" by the federal government, to the point that, at least according to the American Civil Liberties Union (ACLU), such organizations as People for the Ethical Treatment of Animals (PETA) and the antiabortion group Operation Rescue might be deemed terrorist under certain circumstances. Should a mere supporter of PETA, Greenpeace, or Operation

Rescue—knowing nothing, and almost certainly disapproving, of future violent actions taken by individual members of such a group under its name—be subject to such a radical punishment as loss of American citizenship? Under this provision, as Yale Law School professor Jack Balkin notes: "[G]ive a few dollars to a Muslim charity Ashcroft thinks is a terrorist organization and you could be on the next plane out of this country."[3] A harder state seems difficult to imagine.

At one level, in its rolling back of protections offered to Americans over several decades, the Patriot Act II reads like the Justice Department's final revenge for the 1960s, a sort of attempt to purge its own "Vietnam syndrome." In the wake of the FBI's COINTELPRO spying on political activists in the 1960s and 1970s, along with similar efforts by police departments around the country, courts required that the FBI and police authorities place strict limits on such surveillance activities unless they received specific judicial approval for these measures. Most of those safeguards would be rolled back in Patriot Act II, at least for terrorist activities—but terrorist activities and support have now been so broadly defined that the possibilities for surveillance seem considerably broader than they once did.

Dead on Arrival So Why Is Patriot Act II Important?

Opposition to the Patriot Act II was immediate and vociferous. Resistance came first from civil liberties organizations, but, as with the original Patriot Act, Total Information Awareness (TIA), and some other post–September 11 initiatives, the civil libertarians were quickly joined by a host of conservative organizations and a range of federal lawmakers. Shortly after the draft of the Patriot Act II was released, *New York Times* conservative columnist William Safire (in turn quoted by the alliance-building ACLU) termed the draft an "abomination," saying that "Justice's aim is to avoid judicial or Congressional control."[4] And Bill O'Reilly, a conservative commentator on the Fox News Network, expressed anger at the Patriot Act II and particularly the "DNA bank."[5] A number of congressional Republicans expressed views ranging from skepticism to outright opposition.

The strategy was clear. As the ACLU's own specialist on the Patriot Act II pointed out: "[T]he Attorney General should know that if he goes forward with Patriot Act II as written, he'll be facing opposition from every point on the political spectrum."[6] That threat was backed up when dozens of organizations signed a letter to Congress urging Congress to refuse to pass Patriot Act II. They included the expected liberal groups but also more conservative organizations such as the American Conservative Union, the Gun Owners of America, American Baptist Churches USA, and Americans for Tax Reform. Timothy Edgar of the ACLU acknowledged to the *Atlanta Journal-Constitution* what the newspaper termed an "unlikely coalition," noting that "our alliance has been one of the strongest sources of political muscle in this post Sept. 11 world."[7] The ACLU, led by Anthony Romero, even took to prominently cataloging "conservative voices against Patriot Act II" on its web site—including such conservative icons as Bob Barr, Paul Weyrich, Grover Norquist, Arlen Specter, Bill O'Reilly, Larry Klayman of Judicial Watch, and others.

So in one sense the Patriot Act II is important not because it is currently in danger of being enacted as a whole but because it has shown once again the power of right-left alliances in the debate on antiterrorism policy. But Patriot Act II is also important because in two different ways it is not dead. First, few on the right or left seem to doubt that a substantially similar version of the bill will be introduced in the tragic event of another major terrorist attack on American soil. Second, in the meantime, the Justice Department has quietly begun importing provisions of the draft bill into other legislation or directing those provisions toward the states for implementation. In early May 2003, for example, the Senate adopted a measure allowing the government to use secret warrants to conduct surveillance on the so-called lone wolves, terrorists (or terrorist supporters) whose affiliation to a known terrorist organization cannot be proved. That provision was successful partly because the Justice Department knew how to form alliances too: in this case, "lone wolf" warrants had the support of the powerful Democratic senator Charles Schumer as well as some Republican lawmakers.[8]

Another example of how Patriot Act II provisions have found their way into other laws is the previously mentioned inclusion in the draft bill of a proposal to bar public disclosure of industrial "worst case scenario" documents prepared for the Environmental Protection Agency. The homeland security bill passed by Congress and signed into law by the president in 2003 contains a provision similar to that in the Patriot Act II but perhaps even broader: It enables the government to refuse to disclose to the public, under the Freedom of Information Act, information on the protection of "critical infrastructure" considered "sensitive" by the industry groups required to produce it, significantly restricting the public's right to information and promoting secrecy without effective oversight.[9]

The unsanctioned release of a draft of the Patriot Act II is important for another crucial, if ironic, reason. The release and the firestorm of protest that followed provided valuable information to the Justice Department and the White House on which elements of the draft might be enactable and which were "dead on arrival." In turn that understanding may have assisted prioritization of some of the many diverse elements in the bill. Seven months after the Center for Public Integrity posted the draft act on its web site, the president chose three elements of the Patriot Act II agenda to emphasize, prioritize, and promote during a speech marking the second anniversary of September 11 delivered at the FBI Academy in Quantico, Virginia. Those three elements were subjecting a wider range of terrorism offenses to the death penalty, including political advocacy, that may unintentionally result in the loss of life (originally section 411 of Patriot Act II); strengthening the Justice Department's authority to use "administrative subpoena" power and National Security Letters to seize records without judicial hearings (originally sections 128 and 129 of Patriot Act II); and limiting the role of judges in granting bail to terrorism detainees so that the government can deny bail to terrorism detainees (section 405 of Patriot Act II).

It may be, in fact, that these proposals are the "real" Patriot Act II—the core of what the government believes it needs and wants to fight terrorism, with the remainder of Patriot Act II left for debate and, perhaps, a future tragedy. And in certain cases—as in the expansion of administrative subpoena authority, these are steps that Congress resisted when it adopted the original Patriot Act in late 2001 but that the executive branch still wants. Even with these more limited priorities, however, conservative groups and members of Congress, including Patriot Act supporters such as Senator Arlen Specter of Pennsylvania, voiced their skepticism, and the *New York Times* opined that "none of these tools are necessary to fight terrorism, and each threatens to infringe on the civil liberties of Americans."[10] None of this appeared to faze the Justice Department, which seems to have continued the process of importing Patriot Act II provisions into other legislation. In the fall of 2003, a drug control bill proposed in Congress, the

Victory Act, incorporated several Patriot Act II elements, including expanded powers to take records and wiretap.[11]

CAPPS II Institutionalizing an "America of the Watched"

What is being developed as the "nation's largest domestic surveillance system"[12]—a computerized system of melding government and private records to investigate and evaluate terrorist potential among tens of millions of air passengers, airline workers, and other transportation employees—and the accompanying complaints and suits alleging racial and political profiling of passengers allowed on board passenger planes since September 11, 2001, have rapidly become significant domestic and international issues.

The original Computer Assisted Passenger Prescreening System (CAPPS) was developed in the 1990s by the Federal Aviation Administration to gauge the likelihood of terrorist activity by airline passengers and prevent terrorist incidents. It profiled air passengers on a number of criteria, including the use of cash to buy air tickets and the purchase of one way tickets. The original CAPPS program admittedly did not work well, in one well-known incident flagging even a congressman, who then reportedly joined a frequent flier program to stay off the watch lists.[13] The program signaled six of the nineteen September 11 terrorists, but it also flagged another sixty-five thousand travelers that day—making effective searching of all sixty-five thousand (plus six terrorists) impossible.

Some members of minority groups have firmly believed that CAPPS, its interpreters and enforcers, or airline security staff implementing CAPPS racially profiled Muslims, African Americans, and others, pulling them aside for searches and questioning them on a disproportionate basis.[14] Political dissenters also charged, and government documents seemed clearly to show, that politically based "no fly lists" drawn up by the FBI, CIA, and other agencies and enforced by the Transportation Security Agency were in effect. Suits to halt such racial and political profiling were initiated in 2002 and 2003.[15]

The next generation of CAPPS screening, called CAPPS II, was initiated after the September 11 attacks by the new Transportation Security Administration (TSA). As a general proposition, government screening of air passengers to safeguard them and air workers from terrorism is clearly defensible. CAPPS II is designed to add data from within and outside the air passenger system to the threat evaluation process—such data as government and business records (available to the government under the Patriot Act), credit files, and other information. The data would be used to sort passengers; in one early version, "Greens would be allowed to pass. Yellows would be subject to heightened scrutiny. And, Reds would presumably be pulled aside and detained."[16] The government's plan did not end with air travelers: TSA intended that the program would eventually investigate and assess "truckers, railroad conductors, subway workers and others whose transportation jobs involve the public trust" and locate criminal offenders as well as terrorist suspects. Senior government officials have called CAPPS II "the most important security tool we have in our arsenal."[17]

Problems of design, experimentation, and opposition have plagued CAPPS II from virtually the moment it was initiated. A plan to test a prototype of the system during the 2002 Winter Olympics failed due to delays in developing the program and liability concerns.[18] Rationales for the program have also changed rapidly. At one point, CAPPS II was being designed to identify terrorists by the vague measure of whether air travelers were "rooted in the community."[19] Later, the rationale became both more targeted and arguably even more difficult—directly identifying potential terrorists. And opposition has dogged the program from the beginning: from suspicious, reluctant, even recalcitrant airlines that were concerned because of air travelers' negative reaction to the collection and interpretation of personal data. A host of organizations supporting privacy rights, along with business travelers' groups and others, united against the program and effectively delayed its development.[20] They were joined by the American Conservative Union and others also concerned for the privacy rights of individual Americans and by the powerful lobbies of air travelers in general and business travelers.

The problems only accelerated. An intelligence official was named to head and jump-start the project in November 2002, but that also led to increasing concern in the civil liberties community about access to wide-ranging data and the uses that might be made of that access.[21] In early 2003, the TSA settled on military contractor Lockheed Martin Corporation to design and construct CAPPS II, and the press identified Delta Airlines, IBM, and others as initial cooperators in testing a prototype.[22] Delta's plans to share air passenger data for use in the development of CAPPS II immediately ran into a buzz saw of opposition, led by business travelers, corporate travel managers, and travel agencies that the weakened U.S. airlines have worked hard to retain in the difficult days since September 11.[23] Complaints to and about Delta, including a Boycott Delta web site, prompted Delta to pull out of the testing of the CAPPS II prototype. Critics continued to charge that CAPPS II is a blunt instrument using highly intrusive information from commercial and government databases that may be replete with error and is thus an overintrusive tool unlikely to fulfill the tasks set for it. Civil libertarians termed it a "blacklist of airline passenger[s], who . . . have a scarlet letter of 'potential threat' forever imprinted in their commercial and government data fingerprints," one perhaps fatally dependent on an encouragement of racial and other profiling.[24] Even the president's Office of Management and Budget (OMB) seemed skeptical. "I have a huge spotlight on that project," noted a senior OMB official to a congressional committee. "If we can't prove it lowers risk, it's not a good investment for government." And in the spring of 2003, the European Union (EU) noted that CAPPS II was also intended to screen and rate foreign (including European) travelers coming into the United States by air. In perhaps its most pointed critical statement against any of the post–September 11 antiterrorism measures in the United States other than the Guantanamo detentions, the EU warned against screening European travelers to the United States with data gathered from European sources, noting that "access to data banks in the European Union would raise issues with EU data-protection legislation."[25]

Until the announcement that planning for the Patriot Act II was under way, it was CAPPS II that seemed to galvanize perhaps the widest array of opposition to a post–September 11 government initiative that had a significant impact on civil liberties. The coalition of opposition to aspects of CAPPS II— civil libertarians, prominent conservatives and conservative organizations, corporate travelers, information privacy and other organizations[26]—and the problems they identified in the planned system caused a U.S. senator to note that the CAPPS II debate might symbolize "the beginning of a debate of how our country can fight [terrorism] ferociously, without gutting civil liberties."[27]

In response to these and other criticisms, TSA officials seemed to pull back from some of their more expansive plans in 2003. They said that the CAPPS II program would not draw personal information into its computers, with the exception of names and "a few other details, such as telephone numbers and addresses."[28] The initial government plan to retain CAPPS II data for fifty years has now supposedly been scaled back, but the government also announced that data derived from the examinations would be used to track and arrest suspects in nonterrorism offenses as well, such as suspects in violent crimes.[29]

Under new plans announced in August 2003, the TSA said that CAPPS II would proceed with the collection of basic information, cooperation with private "data aggregators" (private companies with huge data mining capabilities) to "authenticate" the traveler, and calculation of a "risk assessment score" based on secret data and secret criteria.[30] TSA's director estimated that 3 to 4 percent of air passengers would undergo heightened inspection. Civil liberties groups, conservative organizations, lawmakers, newspapers, and others continued to raise complaints of secrecy; ineffectiveness; the inability to stop expanding use of the data collected; a lack of due process in the revised CAPPS II procedures; the likely racial, ethnic, and political discrimination in the process; and, not least, the next step in the increasing privatization of national security efforts.

Despite the criticism, the government never withdrew its plans for an expanded CAPPS system. The European Union gave temporary permission for European airlines to share passenger data with the U.S. government in early 2003, and a series of canceled flights on security grounds from Paris, London, and Mexico City at the end of 2003 gave further urgency to the U.S. government's plans to screen all air travelers using the more detailed CAPPS II system.[31] By late 2003, plans were in place to begin transferring European air passenger data into TSA systems, over the continued opposition of many European citizens and lawmakers, after the U.S. government reduced the breadth of its demands for information and agreed to shorten the retention of information.[32]

In September 2003, the American airline JetBlue admitted that it had provided data on as many as five million air passengers to a Department of Defense contractor, in violation of Jet-Blue's own guarantees to customers, sparking angry complaints and lawsuits.[33] Faced with these problems and criticisms, Congress put a hold on the CAPPS II program in late September 2003, at least until TSA could show that CAPPS would not result in "a large number of false positives" and that there would be an "internal oversight board" to scrutinize the program, "sufficient operational safeguards to reduce . . . opportunities for abuse," and no "privacy concerns with the technological architecture of the system."[34]

In early 2004, the Transportation Security Administration once again announced that it planned to begin use of CAPPS II to screen airline passengers. To pacify corporate and frequent travelers, CAPPS II would now be supplemented by a smaller program, "Trusted Traveler," that would speed business and frequent fliers through security checkpoints in exchange for advance provision of substantial personal data. The reinitiation of CAPPS II came under immediate attack from civil liberties and conservative groups, as well as newspaper editorialists, with assertions that it would be ineffective and vulnerable to manipulation, subject Americans and others to "check[ing] against secret government intelligence databases," and discriminate against minorities and the poor, who may have less financial data available for "aggregation" and in favor of richer travelers.[35]

In January 2004, in a virtual repeat of the earlier JetBlue debacle, documents released to the Electronic Privacy Information Center showed that Northwest Airlines had provided air passenger data to the government in 2001 in violation of denials and pledges it had made to its many customers. Unlike JetBlue, Northwest defended its actions as "a duty and an obligation."[36] Airline executives met quickly to discuss a "privacy protocol"—as well as joint plans to turn over passenger data records to the government for use in the CAPPS II screening system.[37]

In the spring and summer of 2004, privacy issues continued to slow the implementation of CAPPS II air passenger screening, though transportation security officials insisted that the program would eventually go into effect. European and American officials signed an agreement on the provision of European air passenger data for use in CAPPS II screening in May 2004, the result of long and difficult negotiations and amid continuing and strong opposition in Europe to providing air passenger data to American security agencies. And the "registered traveler" program, intended to speed frequent and business travelers through airport security after prior provision of personal data, went into experimental implementation in the early summer of 2004.[38]

Operation TIPS A Program Crashes & Burns

The Terrorism Information and Prevention System (known as Operation TIPS) was initiated by the Justice Department in early 2002 to enable truckers, postal workers, utility workers, shipping and port workers and officers, bus and subway workers, and others—the "millions of American workers who . . . are in a unique position to serve as extra eyes and ears for law enforcement"—to inform the federal government of "suspicious and potentially terrorist-related activity" through a centralized hot line.[39] These tips would be reported to the federal government through a national volunteer network known as the Citizen Corps, established by the government and announced by the president in the 2002 State of the Union address. That information, in turn, would be transmitted to other federal, state, and local authorities for whatever action they thought necessary.

Operation TIPS was initially portrayed as an amalgamation and expansion of a number of other federal and state reporting hot lines, including the federal Customs BeAlert, Coast Watch, Highway Watch, and Financial Crimes Enforcement Network programs; Michigan's River Watch initiative; the Massachusetts Transit Crime Watch; and four hot lines operated by the federal Bureau of Alcohol, Tobacco, and Firearms (ATF). Yet it would also have been considerably broader, expanding those efforts while adding postal, utility, and other workers who work primarily in residential neighborhoods to a national informant network.

TIPS came under concerted attack almost immediately. Liberal and conservative legislators, state officials, editorial writers, columnists, and advocacy groups denounced it as a serious invasion of privacy, creating incentives for citizens to spy on each other and to engage in ethnic and racial profiling. Such unverified, unanalyzed information, phoned in to the federal government, would in turn be retransmitted without verification, analysis, or controls to law enforcement authorities for investigation or action. Nor was the program necessary, according to the critics, for there are regular and effective channels through which citizens can report suspicious activities to law enforcement authorities. As the *Washington Post* put it in a scathing editorial: "Police cannot routinely enter people's houses without either permission or a warrant. They should not be using utility workers to conduct surveillance they could not lawfully conduct themselves."[40]

The real tipping point came when the conservative majority leader of the House of Representatives, Dick Armey, and a number of conservative and libertarian organizations and individuals also weighed in against the TIPS plans in the summer and early fall of 2002. They included the Rutherford Institute, the Cato Institute, the *Washington Times*, Phyllis Schlafly, *Reason Magazine*, and other proponents of a libertarian conservatism with some significant influence in Washington, raising their voices in often blunt and angry terms that made negotiations with the Justice Department difficult if not impossible. The Rutherford Institute's John Whitehead called TIPS "an absolutely horrible and very dangerous idea. It's making Americans into government snoops. President Bush wants the average American to do what the FBI should be doing."[41] *Reason Magazine* called it "Stalinoid snitching."[42] That powerful alliance of convenience between the libertarian and conservative right and civil liberties groups helped to force a government retreat within months. In July, the U.S. Postal Service announced that it would not participate in the TIPS program despite a request from the new Department of Homeland Security.[43] Even several metropolitan utility companies announced that their workers would not participate, citing potential danger to utility workers if they were perceived as police informants.[44]

The Justice Department responded weakly, first announcing that postal and utility workers would not be included. On the defensive, the department said that it "never intended that workers calling the hot line would report on anything other than publicly observable activities" and announced that the hot line number would not be made available to "any workers, including postal and utility workers, whose work puts them in contact with homes and private property."[45] That failed to quell the outrage. TIPS rapidly became a sort of political poster child for allegations of overextension of government power and in mid-July, House majority leader Dick Armey inserted language blocking the TIPS program in the markup of the bill to create the Department of Homeland Security.[46] After Armey declared his opposition and inserted blocking language in the House version of the Homeland Security authorizing legislation, TIPS was probably already destined for a slow death. Its gradual descent became free fall when the online journal salon.com reported that the Justice Department was referring TIPS calls to Fox Television's "America's Most Wanted" hot line. Liberal and conservative forces also opened a new front, blasting the government's plans to turn over TIPS information and its transmission to other federal and state authorities to a nongovernmental private organization, the National White Collar Crime Center, in what the Rutherford Institute called an attempt to "get around the Fourth Amendment and the Freedom of Information and Privacy Act." And the dangers of mistaken informant reports were vividly reemphasized after three medical students, all Muslims, were held in Florida after a day-long search through two states, solely based on the telephone call of a Georgia woman who thought she heard threatening words. The Council on Muslim-American Relations explained the broader lesson: "There's a problem when you basically deputize everyone in America. Does a person reading the Koran in the airport, or a man wearing a skullcap, constitute suspicious activity? Where does it leave us?"[47]

In the late summer and early fall, TIPS seems to have shifted rapidly from an avowed cornerstone of the government's post–September 11 antiterrorism strategy into a pawn available for sacrifice. On November 20, 2002, the House of Representatives ended Operation TIPS through a provision in the Homeland Security Act, an urgent priority of the administration that established the Department of Homeland Security and reorganized government security planning and operations. TIPS appeared dead in the form originally presented to Congress and the American people.

The New Devolution Strategy From National TIPS to Highway Watch, Airport Watch, Eagle Eyes, & Other Programs

But was Operation TIPS dead in its entirety? In a pattern repeated in other unsuccessful post–September 11 programs, this failed national initiative seemed to be reborn in other guises. Both before and after Dick Armey banned the TIPS program, the federal government began rechanneling support for components of the TIPS program to willing industry counterparts, states, and the military, working with enthusiastic partners and seeking to narrow the divide with anti-TIPS conservatives by decentralizing informant-related programs to local levels. In this strategy, the administration appeared to be following the recommendations of conservative analysts such as Jonah Goldberg of *National Review Online*, who recommended eliminating "'98 percent of all conservative-versus-libertarian arguments' by decentralizing most public policy to the cities and counties."[48]

Industry groups seemed among the more willing. In collaboration with the Aircraft Owners and Pilots Association, the Transportation Security Administration established Airport Watch to engage pilots in reporting "suspicious people hanging around privately owned aircraft."[49] Highway Watch was expanded to Pennsylvania and other states with the support of the trucking industry. Trucking officials sought to dampen potential criticism by noting that the program is "noninvasive" because "citizens on the highway [have] no expectation of privacy."[50] State funds were redirected to state tip lines, or homeland security funds were devolved to the states to set up or expand state tip lines.[51] And there were continuing reports of citizens questioned by state or local police as a result of calls to state tip lines, including questioning about political beliefs.[52]

The Eagle Eyes Program

Even the military became involved in reporting and transmission of informant tips. With the strong support of senior military officers and defense officials, the Air Force Office of Special Investigations (AFOSI) established a nationwide program called "Eagle Eyes" in early 2002. Eagle Eyes is, quite simply, a militarized if smaller version of Operation TIPS: military personnel, families, and willing residents in communities near military bases in the United States and around the world are asked to report suspicious events or people. But the scope of Eagle Eyes was by no means limited to military units. The Office of Special Investigations asked citizens to report "people who don't seem to belong in the workplace, neighborhood, business establishment, or anywhere else. . . . This category is hard to define, but the point is that people know what looks right and what doesn't look right in their neighborhoods, office spaces, commutes, etc., and if a person just doesn't seem like he or she belongs, there's probably a reason for that." The reach was to be as wide as possible. "It's important that this campaign reaches as many people as possible," said an OSI representative, "to include not just military people, but civilian workers, family members, contractors, off-base merchants, community organizations, neighborhoods, you name it."[53] Much as Operation TIPS was intended, "[T]he Eagle Eyes program makes ordinary citizens partners in the War on Terrorism," wrote an enthusiastic newspaper reporter near Barksdale Air Force Base in Louisiana. "Calls are immediately routed to appropriate law enforcement agencies and military commanders for rapid investigation."[54]

Eagle Eyes quickly expanded to Air Force bases around the country. On some bases, such as Altus Air Force Base in Oklahoma, informants were offered a "tips page" on the Internet to report suspicious sightings. None of the Eagle Eyes material available on the Internet in early 2004 warned against racial or ethnic profiling. Nor were informants guided effectively in their choice of reports to avoid the plague of overinclusion—suspecting and investigating too many people. Wright-Patterson Air Force Base in Ohio urged that the following "possible terrorist surveillance activities . . . be reported immediately": "individuals who carry on long conversations on pay or cellular phones" and "joggers who stand and stretch for an inordinate amount of time." Eagle Eyes informants "shouldn't be gun-shy about reporting incidents that could turn out to be innocent behavior. . . . 'We're much less concerned about too much reporting than we are with too little.' "[55]

Such unconfirmed, unverified reports by untrained informants potentially subject to profiling and other bias would not be kept within military boundaries. OSI agents would check out reports, but "at the same time"—before checking for unverified reports—they would be "quickly up-channeled to OSI's central analytical center at Andrews Air Force Base, Md., to compare with other Air Force reports, as well as similar information from the Army, Navy and other federal agencies." Even local law enforcement agencies would be informed of such unverified suspicions by untrained informants: "Suspicious reports are quickly distributed over the Internet, not only to all AFOSI detachments, but also to local and federal law enforcement agencies around the country."[56]

In some areas the program expanded beyond the immediate vicinity of Air Force bases, where there is of course an important and entirely legitimate protection goal. Soldiers at Davis-Monthan Air Force Base in Arizona "decided to harness the untapped patriotism of the vast numbers of military retirees in the surrounding area. They obtained lists of retirees living . . . around the city, then went and knocked on doors, enlisting vol-

unteers to establish neighborhood watches within their zones."
And soldiers at an Air Force installation in northern Michigan
have "taken the 'Eagle Eyes' message to a myriad of local, state
and federal law-enforcement agencies, to include the Michigan
State Police, the U.S. Border Patrol, the Immigration and Naturalization Service, the Customs Service, and many others."[57]
The Eagle Eyes program is also integrated with Talon, an Air
Force initiative undertaken after September 11 to collate and
forward "raw, nonvalidated" reports of suspicious activity
rapidly up the chain of command for analysis and action. Talon
was endorsed by Deputy Defense Secretary Paul Wolfowitz in
early May 2003.[58] Eagle Eyes appeared to remain active in the
spring and summer of 2004.[59]

The Struggle against Total Information Awareness—
& Its Successors

The Orwellian-sounding Total Information Awareness program (originally accompanied by an even more Orwellian sym-
bol depicting a large eye surrounded by the motto "knowledge
is power" in Latin) was the brainchild of former Reagan
national security adviser John Poindexter. Poindexter was
charged and convicted of conspiracy and making false statements to Congress for his role in the Iran-Contra scandal in
the 1980s, though convictions were later overturned on appeal.
He resurfaced in the Bush administration's Defense Department as director of the Total Information Awareness initiative
within the secretive Defense Advanced Research Projects
Agency (DARPA).

Following September 11, Poindexter began building the
infrastructure for gathering an immense array of commercial,
public, and other data on individuals and then using that data
in conjunction with formulas developed by DARPA and its

contractors to match individuals to terrorist profiles.[60] This process was, Poindexter told an industry group in August 2002, "analogous to . . . finding submarines in an ocean of noise—we must find the terrorists in a world of noise. . . . [Terrorists] must engage in transactions and they will leave signatures in this information space."[61] But the critics quickly gathered. William Safire of the *New York Times* pointed out what TIA's "getting the 'data-mining' power to snoop on every public and private act of every American" might mean: a database containing "every purchase you make with a credit card, every magazine subscription you buy and medical prescription you fill, every Web site you visit," and more.[62]

Such a large and complex endeavor required a number of constituent research projects under the TIA banner. Those included Evidence Extraction and Link Discovery, "to automatically extract evidence about relationships among people, organizations, places, and things from unstructured textural data, such as intelligence messages or news reports"; HumanID, which sought "to develop technologies that can detect, recognize, and identify humans at a distance"; Next Generation Face Recognition, to "develop a new generation of facially based biometrics"; and FutureMAP (Futures Markets Applied to Prediction), "to provide DoD with market-based techniques for avoiding surprise and predicting future events." FutureMAP came under early attack—the notion of using futures markets to predict, in a sense almost invest in, terrorist attacks against the United States horrified almost all who learned of it with the exception of some defense personnel and some economists. Congress terminated FutureMAP in July 2003.[63]

Many aspects of the TIA program horrified civil liberties advocates, conservatives, libertarians, the media, members of Congress, and others: the gathering of such extensive information through "data mining" of public and commercial materials, the compilation of that data into dossiers, the preparation of so-called terrorist profiles, and the attempts—likely inaccurate and overbroad—to find citizen profiles that match terrorist profiles.

On some other post–September 11 issues, Anthony Romero, Laura Murphy, and other civil libertarians may have needed to coax or shape an opposition alliance. No such work was needed with Total Information Awareness: parts of the American conservative sector erupted in fury, as did civil libertarians and the liberal community. Poindexter did his program no good by clumsily changing the name and logo from Total Information Awareness to Terrorism Information Awareness. The point was clear: the wrapping might change, but the program was too dangerous to be allowed to proceed, particularly within the Defense Department.

In February 2003, Congress ordered a report on the TIA program and refused to allow the Pentagon to continue TIA research without approval from Congress. That approval would be contingent on the Pentagon showing sufficient protection for federal privacy rights. The Defense Department submitted a lengthy report on the TIA efforts in May 2003 in an attempt to save the program. In September 2003, Congress eliminated funding for most—but not all—of the TIA program and ordered DARPA to terminate its Information Awareness Office. At the same time, Congress allowed a number of TIA research projects ostensibly focused on foreign intelligence to continue.[64]

The Defense Department's inspector general released a report on TIA in December 2003, concluding that "DARPA could have better addressed the sensitivity of the technology to minimize the possibility of any Governmental abuse of power." The inspector general declined to confirm a DARPA request that the report note that "DARPA was not developing a system for domestic law enforcement." Instead, the inspector general noted that senior defense officials "clearly indicated that TIA had potential usage by both the intelligence and law enforcement communities."[65] By the end of 2003, it appeared, Total Information Awareness was history.[66]

But did TIA really fail? In February 2004, the Associated Press reported that some TIA efforts had been shifted to the Advanced Research and Development Activity office in the National Security Agency through an understanding with Congress and that some contracts had been granted to companies earlier associated with the Poindexter TIA effort.[67] In the spring of 2004, a panel of eminent former government officials appointed by Defense Secretary Rumsfeld also found that the Pentagon and many other government agencies were collecting "personally identifiable information on U.S. persons for national security and law enforcement purposes," and vigorously urged stronger privacy protections. A General Accounting Office report found that 52 of 128 federal departments and agencies surveyed were using or planning to use data mining programs, with 131 such programs already being used. The GAO noted that the Defense Department is the largest user of data mining programs in the United States.

In response to the GAO report, Barry Steinhardt, the director of the ACLU's technology and liberty program and a key figure in technology and privacy debates after September 11, noted that "We always knew that the [TIA] program was not the only data-surveillance program out there, but it now appears possible that such activities are even more widespread than we imagined."[68] And there is now growing evidence that one form of TIA has migrated to the states, in another example of the resourcefulness of government and private advocates for post–September 11 surveillance and data mining. Welcome to the Matrix.

The Devolution of Data Mining to the States
The Emergence of the "Matrix"

Just as Congress voted to close down the Total Information Awareness development program, word began to spread of efforts at the state level to mine personal data, to create electronic dossiers on criminals and innocent alike, and to link those records in a national system searchable by police, other state officials, and potentially the FBI and CIA as well. This state-based data mining system is called Matrix, for Multistate Anti-Terrorism Information Exchange, and its rise in 2003 appears to signal a shift of some data mining initiatives from the federal government to the states and the private sector.

Matrix is the result of efforts by a private company, Seisint, and a number of states to make data more easily accessible after the 2001 attacks. The system collects government and criminal data from collaborating states and commercial databases to create detailed portraits of individuals. Data would include driver's license information and pictures, social security information, criminal histories, addresses and telephone numbers, tickets and arrests, family members, neighbors, marriages and divorces, credit information, registered vehicles, business associates, and more—a list not dissimilar to that proposed for collection in the Total Information Awareness program.[69] But, as the ACLU pointed out, mining commercial sources, as Matrix openly intended, would enable the system to collect more detailed data than even the government might be able to obtain, including "purchasing habits, magazine subscriptions, demographic information, and lifestyle categorization."[70] Matrix-cleared private personnel would establish dossiers and search the system for "anomalies" that might point to terrorist activity. The system is powered by a search engine called "Who" that stands "at the core of the 'concept as a national intelligence project'"[71] and is capable, in the ACLU's words, of "the mass compilation of dossiers about citizens, criminal and innocent alike."[72] The Matrix project's private managers at Seisint told potential partners that "[w]hen enough seemingly insignificant data is analyzed against billions of data elements, the invisible becomes visible" and called Matrix inquiries "the equivalent of searching a room full of file cabinets containing 10.8 billion index cards in no particular order, with each card containing 2,100 characters of text."[73]

As mentioned previously, Matrix has its roots in the Florida-based data mining company Seisint. Seisint was founded in 1998 by prominent South Florida businessman Hank Asher, whose own data is worthy of mining: according to a Florida law enforcement report, Asher was strongly suspected of having "piloted five to seven plane loads of cocaine from Colombia to the U.S." in the early 1980s, though he was never arrested.[74] A Florida state report also "raised questions about Asher's alleged involvement in a plot to assassinate former Nicaraguan president Daniel Ortega," according to a Florida newspaper.[75] To complicate this picture further, the former director of the Secret Service, Brian Stafford, joined Seisint in 2003, and publicity forced Asher to leave the Seisint board in August 2003.[76] Yet Asher continues to have strong backers, including former New York mayor Rudolph Giuliani and the director of the Florida Department of Law Enforcement, who said in 2003 that Asher "has done more to facilitate intelligence and information-sharing for police in the country than anyone I've ever known."[77]

The initial Matrix system of linking computers for data mining was donated to Florida law enforcement authorities shortly after September 11 and then broadened as Florida officials brought in at least twelve other states for demonstrations. Before federal money arrived in 2002, Asher reportedly contributed $20 million of his own to develop the system and

provided Matrix data free to the federal government.[78] Fourteen states—Alabama, Connecticut, Georgia, Kentucky,
Louisiana, Maryland, Michigan, New York, Ohio, Oregon,
Pennsylvania, South Carolina, Utah, and Virginia—then were
approached or made initial moves to join the Matrix network
and contribute data. And there have been reports of the signing
of a memorandum of understanding with three more states—
California, Florida, and Texas.[79] State membership in Matrix
has been a constantly moving target as states are approached,
express interest, then join the system or back off under criticism or budgetary constraints.

State law enforcement officials who have used the Matrix
system laud its speed and scope. According to its backers,
Matrix enables police to locate and use information on perhaps
hundreds of databases through one interface. And there is little
doubt that such access is sometimes needed. In one example
cited by Matrix backers, the system would enable police to
"instantly find the name and address of every brown-haired
owner of a red Ford pickup truck" in a twenty-mile radius of a
kidnapping, child assault, or murder—and crimes against children, particularly kidnapping and the need for fast action, are
regularly used as the rationale for deployment of Matrix at the
state level.[80] In truth, who could argue with that use of a computer network by law enforcement?

But Matrix is considerably more than a collaborative state-
based law enforcement data system, and it embodies substantial dangers for privacy and civil liberties. By early 2003 Seisint
boasted that Matrix was the "deepest repository of information
on people and companies in [the] US," with a "core capa-
bilit[y]" of "20+ billion records from 100's of sources."[81] This
was an information awareness program that the federal government could support, and it did—at least to a certain degree.
In August 2003 the *Washington Post* reported that the Depart-

ment of Homeland Security had pledged $8 million for development of Matrix and that the Justice Department was budgeting $4 million as well as computer equipment for a national rollout of the system.[82] According to the Justice Department, the Matrix development would "increase and enhance the exchange of sensitive terrorism and criminal activity information between local, state, and federal law enforcement agencies."[83] Matrix data would also be available to the FBI, potentially to the CIA, and to other federal agencies.

By the fall of 2003, as the federal government became more involved in support for Matrix, it was being explicitly likened to Total Information Awareness. Opposition to Matrix began to strengthen in the summer of 2003, just as Total Information Awareness was being delayed and partly dismantled under congressional mandate. Local newspaper reports, particularly in Georgia and Florida, fueled suspicions and helped to galvanize opposition to the quiet efforts of state officials around the country to join the Matrix network. The ACLU quickly expanded coverage of Matrix on its web site and bulletins and filed state freedom of information act requests in multiple states as well as a federal action seeking details about the system. Conservative activists complained of the potential for privacy intrusions against noncriminals and the potential for misuse of the system, and they drew direct parallels to the Total Information Awareness efforts.[84] In some states, state legislators and governors backed away from the program as its privacy implications came to light and they were scissored by criticisms from both liberals and conservatives.

By November 2003, only seven states—Connecticut, Florida, Michigan, New York, Ohio, Pennsylvania, and Utah—remained of those that had originally expressed interest in Matrix and the others that had joined later. Some of those original states had already decided, under privacy, political, or budgetary pressures, to limit their engagement with Matrix. (It was perhaps ironic that state budget crises resulting from tax cuts, federal mandates, and devolution of federal programs contributed to the inability of some willing states to bring Matrix on board.) Some states—such as Texas and California—attended Matrix meetings but seem never to have formally joined the program. Lynn Rasic, a spokesperson for the New York State Office of Public Security, said that "there's no way the state is going to proceed with this program if it doesn't meet our privacy standards 100% and doesn't have federal funding to support it."[85] Georgia originally agreed to share data with Matrix "for law enforcement investigative or intelligence purposes only" and then sent criminal information (including prison and sex offender data) into the system.[86] But opposition expanded, the *Atlanta Journal-Constitution* publicized and then strongly editorialized against joining the program,[87] opponents noted conflicts with Georgia privacy law, and the state attorney general concurred that those conflicts posed a significant problem for data transfer.[88] At that point the governor of Georgia refused to transfer driver's license, photo, vehicle title, and other information to Matrix.

Alabama, Kentucky, Louisiana, Oregon, South Carolina, Texas, and other states declined to join because of costs (after Homeland Security stopped picking up early expenses) and, in some cases, privacy concerns. Ohio signed the original Matrix agreement but delayed sending data to Matrix after opposition strengthened in the state.[89] Yet it could not be concluded that the program was in grave trouble: By the end of 2003 discussions were under way with other states on joining Matrix, and the seven states that had agreed to join were home to more than a quarter of the American population.[90]

Matrix represents privatization and the development of a public-private partnership in exploiting data mining, dossier building, and use of personal information. In its aggregation of data and planned uses, Matrix is not far from the vision of John Poindexter for the TIA project at the Defense Advanced Research Projects Agency, but there is as yet little evidence of direct linkages between the two activities. The role of privatization and partnership with government is clear: the federal Department of Homeland Security provided startup investment, six states contribute at least some data and benefit from it, and Florida police secure the headquarters facility. However, Seisint is a private company, which diverts some publicity and criticism of efforts that might be focused on entirely governmental institutions.

Yet a curious anomaly of the Matrix program is the relative dearth of federal support—only $12 million was publicly identified by the end of 2003 out of available government funds for homeland security in the hundreds of millions of dollars. The value to the federal government of devolving data mining and employment systems to the states seems unassailable, especially after TIA crashed and burned. But that is a value so far unmatched, according to publicly available information, by the level of federal investment.

In the spring of 2004, the ACLU and journalists uncovered evidence that Matrix's parent company, Seisint, had forwarded 120,000 names of suspected terrorists culled from its Matrix and other databases to federal and state authorities after September 11. Amid new reports of close links between Matrix and the Department of Homeland Security, and that a Matrix precursor had been shown at the White House to Vice President Cheney, FBI Director Mueller, and other top officials in early 2003, opposition to Matrix continued to grow, especially in the states in which the program was most active, including Florida, Ohio, and Michigan.[91]

3

The States & Antiterrorism
Dialogue & Resistance

In the early days after September 11, a number of states moved quickly to enact various forms of strengthened antiterrorism legislation—some expanding the definition of terrorism in state law and strengthening punishments, others adopting new measures on emergencies and public health, and some engaging in vigorous debate about providing law enforcement with new wiretapping and surveillance tools. These moves did not occur in an empty playing field, for a number of states had already begun addressing terrorism-related issues in the 1990s. In Illinois, for example, where several heavily scrutinized Muslim American charitable organizations were based, the legislature had passed a law in 1996 that criminalized solicitation of or providing support for "international terrorism." California had adopted legislation against manufacturing, possessing, using, or threatening to use "weapons of mass destruction" in 1999, as well as against possession of some biological agents.[1]

But the world was different in the early days after the brutal September 11 attacks, and the states rushed toward legislation in response. Some of that legislation was symbolic: a few state legislatures, for example, considered or enacted legislation mandating or strongly encouraging recitation of the Pledge of Allegiance. And some of the legislative initiatives had perhaps less serious civil liberties or political implications than others—such as moves to upgrade some public health, emergency management, state building security, and other areas. And in virtually all states, the desire to join in the struggle against terrorism had to be balanced by the realities of fiscal life.[2]

In these early days, as this chapter shows, civil liberties activists sought to build coalitions with libertarian conservatives and others to delay and, where possible, ameliorate the most draconian aspects of the rush toward new state antiterrorism law. In a number of states this alliance was somewhat successful; in others the early antiterrorist legislative packages passed relatively quickly and easily. In early 2002 the American Civil Liberties Union (ACLU) wrote of "state and local insatiable appetites" for new powers, including expanded wiretap authority and increased surveillance.[3]

But by mid-2002, the haste to enact immediate antiterrorist legislation at the state level began to abate, though in a number of states these battles now turned to crucial issues such as the expansion of state wiretapping authority and conservative forces kept state legislation high on the agenda. The results of this second stage of jockeying over state antiterrorism legislation in 2002 and 2003 were mixed, but in a number of states the coalition of civil liberties, libertarian, and other constituencies held the line against a further resurgence in executive authority—ironically aided by the adoption of national laws that undercut the rationale for an expansion of some state authority.

A number of state legislatures—California, Michigan, and Wisconsin among them—declined to give law enforcement and other state authorities strengthened authority to wiretap akin to that adopted in the federal Patriot Act. The Florida legislature passed an initial wave of antiterrorism legislation but then refused to pass a law that would have forced colleges and universities to report data on adult foreign students to a state police database. Even some provisions requested by Governor George Pataki in New York, home of the World Trade Center, were denied by the New York legislature.[4]

By late 2003 and early 2004, the battles had begun to shift once again. Though conservative forces continued to introduce expanded wiretapping and other legislation, little was emerging in adopted form, partly due to the vigilance of the civil liberties, libertarian, and pro-privacy communities. But state battles now began to focus on the role of state authorities—state police, homeland security bureaus, governors, attorneys general—in implementing federal data mining and surveillance measures that had encountered political roadblocks at the national level because of their threats to privacy and civil liberties. Conservative attempts to further extend the antiterrorism legislative and enforcement agenda have clearly increased and in some cases migrated to the states. These include the Matrix project discussed in chapter 2, a corporate-state partnership data mining program that, in certain ways, succeeded John Poindexter's discredited Total Information Awareness (TIA) initiative, as well as some aspects of the Operation TIPS (Terrorist Information and Prevention System) proposals.

Because of the nationwide focus on the Patriot Act and other federal measures, the intensive efforts around the country to enact and to resist state-based legislation in the wake of September 11 have often escaped notice. State legislative efforts receive little attention in the national press and even from the key civil liberties organizations that are hard pressed even to defend against the expansion of federal law and policy. And so the strategies and efforts to block, water down, or ameliorate some of the more intrusive state proposals fall to local coalitions of civil liberties organizations, interested legislators of various views, committed citizens, and local newspapers. Sometimes those coalitions are strong, and sometimes they are weak.

This chapter discusses these important developments in state-based antiterrorism policy by looking carefully at the experiences of three politically important, highly populated and diverse states in which these battles have been waged— California, Michigan, and New York. It then draws some initial conclusions about the scope and progress of state-based antiterrorism law and policy and the coalitions that have banded together to slow or stop their advance.

Defining a Field of Battle The Scope of State-Based Antiterrorism Law & Policy

If federal antiterrorism law and policy are broad, complex, and difficult to categorize, state efforts are, if anything, even more unwieldy to discuss. The National Conference of State Legislatures provides one quite useful framework that classifies state antiterrorism laws and proposals into several important arenas, adapted for discussion here.[5]

> *the expansion of provisions for crimes involving terrorism in state criminal laws,* including definitions of broad new crimes involving terrorism and the provision of substantial penalties, including the death penalty in some cases;
> *efforts to improve environment, energy, and transportation security,* including legislation designed to address potential threats to nuclear power plants and water, gas, oil, and power facilities; drivers' licenses and identity concerns; and terrorism in the agricultural sector;
> *legislation in the economic and commercial arena,* including work to improve airports and other transportation facilities;

statutes and policies to strengthen emergency management and the administration and operations of government, including the security of state capitol buildings and other key state institutions; compensation for police and for military reservists; and, certainly most important, the formation or rapid expansion of state offices of homeland security in each of the fifty states;

protection of health, including measures to defend public health institutions and other facilities; efforts to avert bioterrorism; and a series of "emergency health powers acts" that cover disease surveillance, reporting requirements, isolation and quarantine, examination and treatment of certain persons, compulsory vaccination in some cases, public health emergencies, and other issues;

protection against cyberterrorism and defense of information technology and Internet resources, including laws to punish terrorist use of the Internet;

loosening of restrictions on wiretapping and eavesdropping in defense against terrorism; and

legislation intended to strengthen the expression of patriotism, including mandatory expression, which was introduced in a number of states after September 11.

Not all of these areas are equally controversial, and space does not permit discussing them all. Two of the more important areas, each discussed subsequently in state examples focusing on California, Michigan, and New York, are omnibus antiterrorism laws and the proposed relaxations of state wiretapping and eavesdropping laws.

Many of these new or enhanced laws and policies are largely unobjectionable and even necessary under the circumstances as American states adapt to an environment of heightened concern about terrorism. And so, in principle, few would object to regulations or policies that strengthen the security of state capitols and other key government buildings, or that make it less likely that terrorists can obtain drivers' licenses and other useful documents, or that enable states to deal with terrorist-related public health emergencies.

But even the less objectionable elements of the state-based antiterrorist agenda may harbor significant issues. When does the need to strengthen security at key government buildings interfere with the exercise of democratic rights? Already there have been charges that the rationale of protection against terrorism is being used to keep protestors away from federal and state officials, including requirements that wide distances be maintained between nonviolent protestors and the president. When does public health emergency legislation carry with it the danger of political overreaching and overuse of powers? As even the National Conference of State Legislatures—which helped to draft the Model State Emergency Health Powers Act discussed later in the chapter—commented: "[S]ome critics claim the . . . emergency powers go too far and that the act's language is too vague."[6] When do enhancements in tracking identity documents translate into tracking individuals and their activities? When do broad definitions of terrorism in laws designed to prevent "cyberterrorism" come to be used to punish persons exercising free speech rights? In the midst of other, often more pressing, issues, some of the disadvantages and misuses of otherwise unobjectionable state laws and policies are not being fully addressed.

Michigan

Shortly after the September 11 attacks and during the wave of anthrax letters, when the atmosphere was at its most charged, the Michigan legislature passed a statute strengthening penalties for manufacturing, possessing, transporting, or releasing chemical or biological weapons. The attorney general of Michigan, soon to become governor, called implied and false terrorist threats "equivalent to domestic treason" and called for stiff penalties for such activities. Even more important were calls for new laws to allow state enforcement authorities to engage in wiretapping at the state level to investigate suspected terrorism and to obtain evidence about a wide range of other crimes as well.[7] And it was to these proposals that Michigan's civil libertarians, as well as privacy-oriented conservative legislators and activists, quickly turned their attention. "On September 12 of 2001 I would not have taken bets on our being able to stop wiretapping," notes William Flory, who spearheaded the ACLU of Michigan efforts to soften and delay severe new legislation after the terror attacks. "We looked upon every day without a vote as a minor victory. The further out a vote, the more we had the sense we would prevail."[8]

In Michigan and in other states, the early environment for opponents of such wide-ranging proposals was bleak. Five days after the September 11 attacks, the *Detroit News* had blared the headline "America Approves Limits to Liberties."[9] Faced with a "mob mentality . . . taking hold to support something that until now was deemed not necessary in Michigan,"[10] Michigan's civil libertarians and others pleaded for patience and played for time, reaching out to traditional constituencies and the press as well as to others concerned with the freedom implications of potentially draconian state legislation.[11] Republicans were quoted freely—Senator Chuck Hagel of Nebraska, for example, who said that "if we abandon the liberties we cherish, the terrorists will have won."

The major push was to allow state-based wiretaps of telephones and surveillance of online activity, long desired by Michigan prosecutors and police and long denied by the Michigan legislature. The wiretap and surveillance proposals would have directly allowed the state police to tap the telephones of suspected criminals and given the state attorney general authority to allow local prosecutors to wiretap suspects with court approval. Opponents charged that the motivation for the bill was not terrorism. "You have been trying to get this legislation through since 1973," a criminal defense attorney told Michigan's Senate Judiciary Committee. "We're not talking about going after terrorists here. We're talking about going after drug traffickers."[12] After active debate about the wiretap provisions,[13] they died on the floor of the Michigan House at the end of the 2002 legislative session.

The alliances built between civil liberties organizations and conservative privacy activists, many from a libertarian bent, were crucial to this victory. As William Flory explains: "[T]here were contacts with some Republicans before September 11, more with libertarians than with the social conservatives. . . . They were concerned about the impact of greatly expanded police powers. They recognized that the ACLU would be a valuable ally. . . . There was a different set of allies against the wiretapping provision than against the terrorism bill—a broader coalition, including some more directly concerned with the privacy issues in the wiretapping bill. One key argument was that there was already a federal wiretapping statute, and a feeling that was enough and a state effort wasn't needed. . . . [And] people pointed to the Patriot Act and said that had taken care of a lot of the problems."[14]

A wide range of other proposals was put forward by state officials. The proposed legislation was designed to narrow public disclosure laws to keep more government documents confidential, particularly documents related to search warrants and the affidavits necessary for them. The materials in question were not limited to terrorism-related activities but included warrants for drug and other offenses. The proposals would have allowed seizure of the assets of convicted terrorists, mandated background checks on criminal records for students in flight schools, provided the state Secretary of State with the power to deny driver's licenses to undocumented or illegal aliens, and established or expanded penalties for supporting or hindering the prosecution of terrorism.[15]

The press emerged as an important brake on the march of antiterrorism legislation in Michigan, especially the expanded wiretapping provisions. State newspapers editorialized that the federal government should be left to handle antiterrorism issues and expressed anxiety about the wiretapping bill. "It would have been considerably more difficult to pull a coalition together without the media," notes Flory. "Most media took the position that there was no rush to pass legislation, there should be careful consideration before enactment. . . . And in the aftermath of the Patriot Act . . . there was a concern about the impact on investigative journalism that caught their attention."[16]

The civil liberties community, conservatives, and the press also criticized a proposal in the Michigan Anti-Terrorism Act, tabled in 2002, that would have broadly defined a new crime of terrorism so that even "a public protestor in a demonstration that goes awry could be charged as a terrorist." Civil libertarians warned that existing crime statutes would easily cover terrorist actions and that "the threat of life imprisonment is an unlikely deterrent for people who are willing to engage in suicide attacks."[17] That the proposed bill's definition of terrorism allowed the punishment of activity intended to "influence or affect the conduct of government or unit of government" particularly worried civil libertarians, gay and lesbian groups, and others. The ACLU of Michigan called the definition of terrorism in the proposed Michigan Anti-Terrorism Act "even worse than [in] the new federal law," the Patriot Act. Similar objections based on vagueness and severity were raised to the new crimes of furnishing criminal assistance or material support to terrorists and of making a terrorist threat.[18]

The Michigan situation was complicated by the presence of a large Arab and Muslim community in Detroit, Dearborn, and other communities and by protests against discrimination toward that community. Michigan became the site for the first judicial challenge in the country to the closing of immigration hearings for noncitizens swept up in the post–September 11 crackdown when the ACLU challenged the closing of immigration hearings for Rabih Haddad, a leader in the Ann Arbor Muslim community and the Global Relief Foundation.[19] For the civil liberties community and its allies, the presence of that large population was an advantage. "We were able to point to a specific group that might be harmed by draconian measures," says Flory. "And such a large group gave a degree of leverage. . . . It was hard to ignore the impact on that large a community. It was helpful to have people to speak who were directly impacted."[20]

The final antiterrorism bill stripped out the wiretap and electronic surveillance provisions, a significant victory for the coalition of civil liberties organizations, defense attorneys, and others. There were other victories as well. The provision to prohibit illegal aliens from receiving driver's licenses was dropped from the Anti-Terrorism Act.[21] As mentioned previously, the proposed measure to expand state wiretapping was also dropped from the act. It also retained provisions to maintain secrecy on some government documents that would normally be open under Michigan's open records law—primarily relating to search warrants, including search warrants issued in situations entirely unrelated to terrorism. State authorities put that provision to use almost immediately. In late May, a county drug task force executed a search warrant in a drug case in Howell, Michigan, where only a seventeen-year-old boy was at home at the time. County officials then refused to provide the single mother who lived at the home with the affidavits underlying the search warrant, directly citing the secrecy provisions of the new Anti-Terrorism Act and sparking protests from the city where the raid took place and civil liberties activists. Partly in response to that raid, legislators pushed through a bill in the summer of 2002 making search warrant affidavits available to those searched fifty-six days after they were issued.[22]

The final package of legislation, generally referred to as the Michigan Anti-Terrorism Act, certainly contained largely unobjectionable elements—such as revisions to the state's Emergency Management Act that help communities work together in emergency situations and protection for "vulnerable targets" such as power plants and other infrastructure. While it criminalized "act[s] of terrorism" against the objections of civil libertarians and others, the definition of "terrorism" was reined in, and the law specifically guaranteed that prosecutions would not be permitted against actions protected by the First Amendment. Crimes of aiding terrorists, hindering terrorist prosecution, and making real or hoax terrorist threats were added. Search warrants and their underlying affidavits were made nonpublic information, against the arguments of government openness advocates. The statute of limitations for terrorism-related offenses was eliminated.[23]

In the end, then, the results were mixed, but the strategy of alliance building, full discussion, and delay proved as successful as any approach could have been. As the ACLU of Michigan put it: "[T]he coalition of groups put together by the ACLU . . . significantly helped to slow the process." And the desire for a broad, bipartisan antiterrorism package gave opponents some leverage. Again, as the ACLU noted: "[T]he discussion[s] between the parties gave us the time and opportunity to point out flaws that sent the bills back to the drawing board more than once. The more time that passed between September 11th and the vote . . . the more willing legislators were to question the language and even the necessity of the bills. As a result . . . the language in the new Michigan Anti-Terrorism Act . . . is a far cry from the very frightening original version we saw last fall."[24] In the end, the expanded wiretap authority failed because of a liberal-conservative alliance that included Republican and libertarian lawmakers, the lack of remedies for citizens wrongly wiretapped or put under electronic surveillance to sue the state, and repeated attempts to narrow the wiretap authority by limiting it to specific terrorist threats.[25]

Civil libertarians summarized this struggle in uncharacteristically positive terms. "After September 11, 2001, there were very few people who believed that we would be able to stop anything that was labeled 'anti-terrorist.' They were wrong. Given the sorts of so-called anti-terrorist measures that have been adopted at the national level, we did quite well. The legislation to block illegal immigrants from obtaining drivers' licenses was defeated in the Senate because members were convinced that its impact would reach beyond illegal immigrants. The wiretapping proposal was defeated as an unnecessary and costly idea that would not help to catch terrorists. Even the Michigan Anti-Terrorism Act is a far cry from the USA-PATRIOT Act and is far less threatening that the original version."[26] Different and overlapping coalitions and alliances to oppose diverse elements of the state's agenda were the clear strategy in the Michigan battle and one that seems to have worked as well as could be expected under the circumstances.

The struggle in Michigan against unreasonable antiterrorist measures quieted after the adoption of the Michigan Anti-Terrorism Act, but it did not end. In late 2003, word leaked out that Michigan, Connecticut, New York, Ohio, and Pennsylvania were participating or seriously considering participation in the Matrix data mining and surveillance program discussed previously—the successor to Total Information Awareness in which data mining is devolved to the states through the work of a private corporation. The ACLU immediately filed freedom of information act requests in those states, as well as in Florida and Utah, where the Matrix program is already operating with state support, seeking information on the sorts of data state officials are allowing Matrix to utilize and on how the resulting Matrix files are being used by the states. In December 2003, the Michigan State Police replied to the ACLU, providing some documents and stating that "the MSP currently is not a user of Matrix."[27] But the company operating Matrix has noted in its promotional materials that Michigan has "signed a memorandum of understanding to participate in Matrix"; Michigan officials attended a Matrix briefing on May 8, 2003; and minutes of a Matrix meeting in November 2003 show that, while Michigan may not be a "user" of Matrix, it certainly has contributed data to the effort. At a Matrix Board of Directors meeting in November, Inspector Karen Halliday of the Michigan State Police said that "Michigan has provided sex offender registry data and Department of Corrections data. The state is still working on providing driver's license data."[28] By early 2004, civil liberties groups were pressing for more information from Michigan, state newspapers were inquiring about Michigan's participation in Matrix, and state officials began questioning the program.[29]

New York

Nearly three thousand people lost their lives in New York State in the horrific September 11 attacks, and so the state's executive and legislative responses were, justifiably and understandably, rapid and severe. Within a week of the attacks, New York governor George Pataki had convened a special session of the legislature, and within days the legislature passed two significant antiterrorist measures without hearings, amendments, or significant debate.[30] As a result, New York has one of the toughest state-based antiterrorist legislative frameworks in the country. And New York's governor and many state legislators have sought to further strengthen antiterrorist laws since the passage of that act. That process has been encouraged by continuing antiterror investigations both in New York City and around the state, including the well-known case of the "Lackawanna Six," Yemeni Americans from a community near Buffalo who traveled to Afghanistan; trained with Al Qaeda; and were charged with assisting a terrorist organization, pleading guilty in 2003.[31]

But even in New York, so badly hit by terrorism on September 11, cooler heads and democratic debate have largely prevailed after the initial, severe legislative response to the destruction of the World Trade Center—in significant measure because of the alliances built by civil libertarians and others who have been able to ameliorate the most severe of legislation to emerge after the first rush to punish in the fall of 2001.

The New York antiterrorist act adopted shortly after September 11 defined and provided severe penalties for terrorist crimes. Terrorist crimes were defined as the commission of almost any sort of felony in order to "intimidate or coerce a civilian population, influence the policy of a unit of government, or affect the conduct of a unit of government."[32] And they criminalized a range of terrorist-related threats or support activities, including hindering of prosecution, and expanded the list of executable terrorist crimes in New York.[33]

The governor also sought expanded wiretap authority similar to that proposed by (and granted to) the attorney general in the days after the attacks. The New York State Senate agreed to provide that authority, but the assembly did not act. The governor also sought authority for state officials to initiate "roving wiretaps" and to "eliminat[e] the statute of limitations for terrorist offenses."[34] But, once again, this authority was not granted by the legislature in the difficult fall of 2001. Yet these victories were also tempered by problems, including a weakening in the restrictions placed on the New York City police in investigating groups and individuals that engage in political activity. The loosening of this "Handschu settlement" and a wider role for police investigators interested in advocacy groups and individuals caused substantial concern in 2002 and 2003.[35]

When the Model State Emergency Health Powers Act (drafted for the U.S. government's Centers for Disease Control by the Center for Law and the Public's Health at Johns Hopkins and Georgetown Universities in collaboration with several other organizations) came up for consideration in the New York legislature in the spring of 2002, civil libertarians were ready with a sophisticated response: "Government surely has a great responsibility to prevent and respond to . . . bioterrorism" but sought to soften aspects of the bill in order to avoid "using state police powers in a discriminatory manner to suspend freedoms based upon race or national origin." They sought a narrowing of the act's very broad definition of "public health emergency," which as written might be used not only against bioterrorism but also to isolate or quarantine HIV and AIDS patients, "to coerce and punish the most vulnerable among us." They also sought a tightening of the governor's expansive powers to declare such an emergency and to act during it.

Of particular concern was the power to be granted to the

governor to override almost any "regulatory statute" during a public health emergency and to suspend state business processes. The New York Civil Liberties Union graphically pointed out the ramifications: "Under this grant of authority the governor could summarily override any rule or regulation—privacy protections, the Freedom of Information Law, arrest procedures, incarceration standards. Perhaps, most notably, the provision that permits the government to suspend procedures for conducting state business may well include suspension of the judiciary and the state legislature."[36] Other key problems were the powers granted to the governor during such a public health emergency to undertake medical testing of patients that seemed to be, at least formally, voluntary in nature. But the governor would also be empowered to isolate or quarantine those who refused mandatory testing. Because the act also would allow the governor to suspend state business, including the work of the courts, and even to name "emergency judges," there might well be substantial difficulties in asserting individual rights under this legal framework.

The act also would require health care providers and laboratories to report bioterrorism cases to state health institutions, but this is not actually limited to bioterrorism—under the model act, state public health institutions may require the reporting of "any health condition," as well as personal information, data on pharmacy visits, and prescription information. Civil libertarians opposed this provision, arguing that it "can and should be designed to capture information without personal identifiers, absent a showing the state has an overriding interest in breaching the privacy interest a person would otherwise expect."[37]

In New York, as in many other states around the country, the Model Emergency Health Powers Act ran into a buzz saw of opposition from civil libertarians and conservative and libertarian privacy, legislative, and other groups, even from prominent right-wing libertarian magazines. Even survivalists joined in to oppose legislation drafted by eminent specialists in law and public health. But in the end the implications of the act for privacy, for executive power, for governmental access to personal information, and even for forced isolation and quarantine have spelled delays or amendment for the act in a number of states, including New York. Since 2001 the Model State Emergency Health Powers Act has been introduced, in whole or in part, in most of the states. In a number of those, liberal and conservative forces have pressured state legislatures to weaken quarantine and other elements of the model statute.[38]

Governor Pataki's antiterrorism bill passed one chamber of the New York state legislature in 2002 but failed in the other under concerted opposition from civil libertarians, moderates who believed that expanded federal legislation covered most of what was needed, and conservatives concerned with privacy. In early 2003, Governor Pataki once again moved forward, "ramm[ing] anti-terrorism legislation through the Republican-controlled [State] Senate . . . without a public hearing or even the normal three-day waiting period," according to the *New York Times*. Like the 2002 bill, the 2003 action would have expanded roving wiretap authority to all crimes, established new terrorist-related crimes, and weakened double jeopardy protections and protection against searches without warrants.[39]

But like earlier New York attempts to pass sweeping antiterrorism legislation, the 2003 bill was sharply opposed by a growing coalition of civil liberties groups, moderates, libertarians, trial lawyers, public defenders, and others.[40] They were even joined by the New York State Bar Association, which attacked the proposed bill as "not only an attack on terrorism, but an assault on the criminal justice system."[41] In the end, much of the legislative package failed again, the victim of the opposition coalition, intense political conflict between the governor and senior state legislators, and a Democrat-controlled state assembly.[42] The calls for stronger antiterror legislation were renewed in early 2004, though by March 2004 the road to passage looked no easier than in 2002 and 2003.[43]

President Bush sought to bolster New York's antiterror proposals through an April 2004 visit to Lackawanna, where the Yemeni men had been prosecuted for terror involvement. Yet even in the wake of that visit, the New York governor's proposals for reducing the threshold for convictions by allowing accomplice testimony alone for conviction, a weakening of prohibitions against "double jeopardy," and roving wiretaps remained bottled up in the state legislature—the victim of intense Democratic and civil libertarian opposition and rivalry between the governor and the speaker of the New York assembly. New York's civil libertarians even went on the offensive, calling for New York City officials to begin active oversight of the impact of antiterror measures on the Muslim, Arab, and South Asian populations of New York and detailing numerous instances of detentions and ethnic and religious profiling.[44]

California

As mentioned previously, California had adopted legislation against the manufacture, possession, use of, or threat to use "weapons of mass destruction" in 1999, as well as prohibiting possession of some biological agents. It did not immediately pass a state antiterrorism bill after September 11.[45] California did adopt measures to strengthen the definition of a weapon of mass destruction by including means of transport (such as hijacked aircraft) as a weapon. The state also expanded the range of biological agents considered weapons of mass destruction, made provisions for safeguarding the state capitol, and provided support for New York and California victims of the September 11 tragedies.[46] Most of these initial moves went largely unopposed, although California civil libertarians noted that the "new definition of . . . viruses and microorganisms" was "vague and ambiguous" and punished simple possession.[47]

The real battles came in 2002. In late 2001, California governor Gray Davis proposed expanding the powers of California law enforcement officials to employ so-called roving wiretaps against a broad array of suspected terrorists and also suggested weaker requirements for obtaining regular wiretaps and expanded provisions for surveillance of e-mail. California's civil libertarians lobbied against such provisions, seeking to broaden opposition to the measures. The ACLU of Northern California expressed concern that "the Governor's proposals will weaken judicial supervision of telephone and internet surveillance by law enforcement and . . . lead to the surveillance of many innocent Californians." Even the budget crisis and fears of bioterrorism and duplicative big government found their way into the ACLU's approaches: "California is currently facing a major budget deficit and we would be better served if the governor allocated state funds to help fight bio-terrorism instead of duplicating the federal government's efforts." And the legislation's "marginal" impact on terrorism, but substantial impact on privacy, came under criticism as well.[48]

California's civil libertarians and others opposed to the governor's legislative proposals were assisted by an official opinion issued by California's Office of Legislative Counsel that said that roving wiretaps were "beyond the limited wiretapping authority provided to the states by the federal government."[49] The revised version of the bill eliminated provisions for roving wiretaps and for expanded electronic surveillance. And it added a section requiring prosecutors to notify defendants who were identified through wiretapping before trial or a plea bargain.[50]

Another ten terrorism-related bills were also introduced in the California legislature that year. One would have added terrorism to the "special circumstances" for which a convicted prisoner could be executed. That bill, like most of the others, died in the legislature, the victim of civil liberties organizations, groups opposed to the death penalty, and other adversaries. Civil liberties, public health, and other forces succeeded in defeating bioterrorism legislation, modeled after the Emergency Health Powers Act, that would have allowed for quarantining and other harsh measures.[51]

California's civil libertarians and their allies also played a significant role in national issues arising out of the September 11 attacks and government responses to them. As the federal government and airlines began the alleged profiling of airline passengers, removing some passengers from aircraft and refusing others permission to board, the ACLU of Northern California sued in San Francisco to prevent profiling of passengers of Asian or Middle Eastern appearance. And when Attorney General Ashcroft weakened the guidelines on FBI surveillance of political and advocacy groups, civil libertarians demanded that the state attorney general decline to follow suit at the state level and instead maintain limits on federal, state, and local law enforcement investigations under California's state constitutional right to privacy.[52]

In 2003, as most of the harsher antiterrorism measures failed in the California legislature under pressure from civil liberties organizations and other forces, attention turned to nonlegislative means used by California authorities to track dissidents and antiwar activists. Two such means were of major concern: the bulletins issued by CATIC (the California Anti-Terrorism Information Center) and the CAL/GANG database maintained by the state.

CATIC bulletins to local, state, and national law enforcement and civil affairs bodies were supposed to focus on direct antiterrorism threats. But according to documents obtained by the Associated Press: "[A] large part of what this agency is doing has focused on protest groups rather than terrorists. . . . [One] advisory, issued last December and labeled 'For Law Enforcement Use Only,' analyzed anti-war protests 'in an effort to help law enforcement better understand a new movement that appears to be sweeping the United States and the rest of the world.'"[53]

According to the *Oakland Tribune*, CATIC issued a bulletin to local law enforcement authorities before an April 2003 anti-war protest in Oakland detailing the activities of the organizers, Direct Action to Stop the War. At the demonstration, Oakland police used tear gas and rubber bullets against five hundred antiwar marchers, with about twenty injuries resulting.[54] CATIC apologized for issuing the bulletin, noting that "while the Oakland advisory was sent out under CATIC letterhead, it had nothing to do with terrorism. The way in which the language was used and the way in which the advisory was distributed for the Oakland event was not wise and it's not something we intend to repeat. CATIC does not retain any information about any group or any individual that does not have a bona fide connection to violent activity."[55] This certainly did not allay concerns about the use of CATIC, particularly because the standards seemed merely to be set and enforced within the center rather than supervised from outside.[56]

The CAL/GANG database, established as a way to track gang activity, has long been suspected by civil liberties and other groups as having additional, more political, uses for the state. CAL/GANG authorities have refused to provide any significant information about its scope or use, other than the worrisome indication that ill-defined "affiliates" of gang members, who need not be gang members themselves, are included in the system.[57]

The use of these systems to track and report on dissident and antiwar activity may well have violated both the privacy clause of California's constitution and federal law. In response to a rising level of queries and criticism of state-based surveillance, California's attorney general issued new guidelines in the fall of 2003 that limited surveillance by California law enforcement authorities, including police and other officials working on joint task forces in California with the federal government. Under the guidelines, California police and other authorities may not attend or report on political, educational, religious, or social events without "reasonable suspicion of the existence of a criminal predicate." Gathering information in violation of this standard is, the guidelines state, "a mistake of constitutional dimension."

The new guidelines were generally praised by the ACLU and other groups, but some concern was expressed that police officers might not understand or implement the rules with assistance (or enforcement) from above and that local police, which had local guidelines on surveillance of protest and other groups, would need to revise their guidelines to comply with the new state policy.[58]

Space does not permit a fifty-state survey of post–September 11 antiterrorism law and policy. But there are indications that the stages of antiterrorism policy development, and the role of alliances and coalitions in slowing the adoption of new laws and policies, have applicability well beyond those three important states. For example, in Iowa, a substantially rural state that was considerably further from the attacks than New York and somewhat isolated from the ongoing fear of terrorism in California, even fewer antiterrorism measures were adopted as the same alliance-building strategies were used. After spirited debate in the fall of 2001 over proposals modeled after the strengthened New York measures, the Iowa legislature declined to institute the death penalty for terrorism-related murder—opting for life in prison instead—and, according to the Iowa Civil Liberties Union, "amended . . . legislation at least three more times to address the objections of civil liberties advocates." The Iowa legislature even enacted a provision emphasizing that "picketing, public demonstrations and similar forms of expressing ideas or views" would not be prosecutable under a terrorism label.[59]

The alliances noted in Michigan and other states played a substantial role in slowing and ameliorating the more far-reaching proposals in Iowa as well. "The passage of time has also permitted opposition groups to form coalitions with greater clout," noted Ben Stone, the executive director of the Iowa Civil Liberties Union. "The ICLU formed an unlikely alliance of organized labor, the gun lobby and antiabortion activists to seek additional protections. The result: a narrower [anti-terrorism] law that specifically protects political activities."[60] Stone put the matter even more plainly to the *Des Moines Register:* "We'll sleep with anybody to get a bill passed or stopped," he said. "The most important thing is to preserve civil liberties."[61]

Certainly worries remained. Iowa's civil libertarians were concerned that the definition of terrorism "remains broad enough that [even] a group of teenagers throwing rocks at the school principal's home could be charged with terrorism and face penalties of as long as 50 years."[62] The "unusual alliance" blunting the most severe of the state antiterrorism provisions requires constant guarding—and was considerably less powerful on measures not related to privacy. On the eve of the second Iraq war in early 2003, for example, a proposal to require daily recitation of the Pledge of Allegiance made its way back

to the Iowa legislature; although it was not adopted, civil libertarians could not rely on the pro-privacy alliance to block it.

Lesson from State-Based Antiterrorism Initiatives
& Thoughts about the Future

In some states, the rush toward fairly severe antiterrorism legislation was virtually unstoppable after September 11. Understandably, those states included New York. But state-based
coalitions were surprisingly successful in halting or ameliorating a range of more intrusive responses in a number of other
states. Those successes seemed to continue and expand in 2002
and 2003, as more time passed after the attacks and federal legislation came to cover the field. The executive director of the
ACLU of Michigan put it well: "There has been a momentum
to take away liberty. . . . But as more time passes, across the
political spectrum, voices are saying, 'Whoa'."[63]

One clear lesson of antiterror law and policy at the state
level is similar to the lesson from the situation at the federal
level: the formation of broad coalitions and alliances, ranging
from civil libertarians to conservative privacy and antigovern-
ment activists, libertarians, gun owners, antiabortion activists,
moderate legislators, and even the business community has
been able to blunt some of the worst potential excesses of
antiterrorism legislation.

In Michigan and other states, these broad coalitions have
played a crucial role in blocking executive proposals for expansion of state wiretapping and surveillance authority. In most of
the states such proposals have languished, or they have been
pushed off the legislative agenda through the work of broad,
sometimes disparate, coalitions.[64] In states where more severe
antiterrorism legislation has been blocked or weakened, as in

California, activist coalitions have now had to turn their attention to state action that does not require legislative approval. In
California, where the California Anti-Terrorism Information
Center and the CAL/GANG system were allegedly undertaking overly intrusive surveillance of political protestors well
beyond any reasonable definition of "terrorists," the attorney
general came under broad pressure to limit and regulate state
surveillance—and he did. Those new California guidelines are
not perfect, of course, and their implementation will be
watched carefully by a range of groups in California, but they
represent another partial success of broad-based citizens' coalitions in at least softening post–September 11 responses in state
antiterrorism policy.

The New Devolution Controversial Federal Antiterrorism
Policy Comes down to the States

Beginning in 2002 and accelerating in 2003, some troubled
federal programs began to find their way to the states. The
Matrix project partners states with a Florida-based data mining
company to aggregate and provide access to an exceptionally
wide array of data somewhat reminiscent of the Pentagon's
Total Information Awareness program. It has involved as many
as fourteen states, though now fewer because of public opposition, privacy concerns, and budgetary problems. Matrix has
received some acknowledged federal funding, and as TIA
recedes Matrix will bear watching as one of the largest and
most active governmental efforts to gather and disseminate
personal data to law enforcement for terrorism and criminal
investigations. In a similar pattern, as the federal TIPS program disintegrated under criticism, state-based hotlines have
expanded, industrial groups have come into the picture, and

the military has rapidly expanded its Eagle Eyes informant program. All of these activities are discussed in more detail in chapter 2, but the key point here is that discredited and criticized federal efforts are, in most cases, not fading away. In many cases they have come to life again at the state level, scattered and often hidden until the press or civil liberties organizations have brought them to light, demanded information, and led coalitions of opposition at the state level.

4

Antiterrorism & the Nonprofit Sector

September 11 deeply affected the American nonprofit sector. The immediate aftermath of the attacks saw an extraordinary outpouring of giving and charitable activity. According to one survey conducted in early October 2001 for Independent Sector, the umbrella organization of America's nonprofits, 70 percent of Americans contributed money, blood, or volunteer time to help in the wake of the terrorist attacks. Over $1.2 billion was contributed for September 11 relief in less than a month and several billion dollars more by the end of 2001.[1] The events of September 11 and their aftermath also severely tested the capacity and judgment of some nonprofit organizations, particularly in an era when donors are more closely scrutinizing the activities of groups to which they have contributed.[2]

Communications, coordination, the disbursal of funds in an effective manner, overlapping philanthropic activities, and the accountability of organizations for the disbursal of funds—all these were very real problems for the American nonprofit sector in the weeks and months after September 11. In a time of widespread giving and voluntarism, America's nonprofits were the chosen route of most citizens. Although a few nonprofits, such as the American Red Cross, which was accused of retaining funds for longer term relief activities when many donors thought their funds would be used for relief directly associated with September 11, are still trying to regain the public's trust,[3] most emerged with enhanced reputation as citizens watched their effective activities in New York and beyond. But September 11 also brought to the surface long simmering issues about the accountability of nonprofit organizations—to donors, to the public, and to their recipients—and reignited questions of how to ensure that public accountability.[4]

The White House, Congress, the Justice Department, and Homeland Security officials have extolled the role of nonprofits in responding rapidly to human needs after the 2001 tragedy and have praised them for their creative and strategic responses to such longer term issues as the rebuilding of small businesses, arts organizations, and civil society in lower New York after the physical, psychological, economic, and political devastation of the attacks. At the same time, nonprofits have come well within the net of federal and state governments' investigation and prosecution of suspect terrorists and terrorist organizations. Several major Muslim charities that allegedly provided funds to support terrorism in the West Bank, Gaza, Afghanistan, and elsewhere have been shuttered, their assets frozen, and their leaders prosecuted in highly public cases on charges of financial support for terrorists. Perhaps even more worrisome is that a broad swath of American charitable organizations working abroad has had to contend with stricter rules on American overseas giving that were promulgated following the attacks to prevent charitable funds from winding up in the hands of terrorists or supporting terrorist activities overseas. And all American charitable and philanthropic organizations, like much of American society, remain subject to the Patriot Act and other antiterrorism legislation enacted since late 2001.

Charities & Terrorist Financing

Charities are the best cover. They do good works with one hand and provide money and cover for terrorists with the other hand.
—*U.S. official quoted in the* New York Times, *June 14, 2002*

As government investigations of terrorism and terrorist organizations went into high gear immediately after the September 2001 attacks, charitable organizations—and particularly Muslim charities—were among the very first investigative targets. For years, there had been federal and state investigations of Muslim charities amid charges that donated funds were leaving the United States and finding their way into the coffers of terrorist organizations in the Middle East and South Asia. In December 2001, the federal government raided three major Islamic charities—the Benevolence International Foundation, the Global Relief Foundation, and the Holy Land Foundation for Relief and Development—and froze their assets, charging that the charities' funds were being funneled to terrorist organizations including Hamas, Islamic Jihad, and Al Qaeda.[5] These three groups, and others, had long been under federal and state investigation on suspicion of supplying funds to terrorist organizations.[6] But September 11 provided the understandable catalyst for intensifying investigations of these and other groups, and eventually for closing them down, as the government's attention turned to shutting off sources of terrorist financing in the United States.

The closing of major Islamic charities and continuing investigations into Islamic charitable activities seem to have had a chilling effect on organized charitable activity in the Muslim community.[7] The government's actions provoked angry responses from Muslim public policy organizations, legislators, and some newspapers alleging that the government was engaging in discriminatory investigation and prosecution of Muslim organizations.[8] In response, the broader charitable and nonprofit sector, a powerful force in Washington, abandoned the organizations that had been closed and frozen by the government but also—in perhaps a more serious lapse—virtually ignored some real issues in the government's handling of the Muslim charities. The nonprofit sector organized and channeled billions of dollars in giving after September 11 but remained largely frozen in policy paralysis as Muslim charities were investigated and closed. America's nonprofits and their lobbying organizations were practically asleep with regard to thinking through the hard public policy issues of treatment of nonprofits suspected of financing terrorist groups. They would awaken from that slumber only when the sector's direct interests were threatened by the imposition of new potential restrictions on overseas funding in November 2002, limitations that went far beyond a few charities serving the Muslim community to affect some of America's most wealthy and powerful nonprofit institutions.

Benevolence International Foundation

Prior to federal raids and freezing of its assets in December 2001, the Benevolence International Foundation was among America's largest and most active Islamic charities. Headquartered in Illinois, Benevolence collected more than $3.6 million in public contributions in 2001, had $1.7 million in assets, and operated from offices in Chicago, Bosnia, the Republic of Georgia, and seven other countries.[9] Benevolence was frozen based on charges that its charitable funds were being channeled to terrorist organizations in Chechnya, Bosnia, and elsewhere. Shortly after the government's actions, Benevolence sued the government seeking to lift the freeze on its assets, denying that it supported terrorist activities. The government then arrested the foundation's director, Enaam M. Arnaout, in April 2002, charging him with perjury in the foundation's court filings against the government for denying that it supported "people or organizations known to engage in violence, terrorist activities or military operations of any nature."[10] Arnaout would be held in solitary confinement for much of the next sixteen months.

The federal government, under increasing criticism in the Muslim community and Congress for focusing law enforcement's attention on Muslim organizations, took pains to distinguish the three foundations from their supporters. "The Benevolence International Foundation was supporting violence secretly," the U.S. Attorney in Chicago told the *New York Times*. But "persons who gave money to the B.I.F. were victims, not criminal. Today's charges seek to vindicate, not frustrate, the noble intentions of the vast majority of donors, mostly Muslim Americans, who thought they were giving help to needy causes."[11] The government also released information intended to tie leadership of Benevolence to Ramzi Yousef and others jailed for the bombing of the World Trade Center in 1993, as well as to Al Qaeda and Osama bin Laden.[12]

As the struggle over Benevolence continued, a federal magistrate first declined to dismiss the perjury charges against Benevolence and its director, on the strength of government information indicating Benevolence aid to Chechen rebels and terrorist groups in Bosnia and links to bin Laden and other Al Qaeda leaders,[13] while Benevolence continued to deny "knowingly provid[ing] support" to Al Qaeda. Three months later, however, the government's perjury case against Benevolence and Arnaout was dismissed by a federal judge in Chicago because the statements had been made in court filings not subject to the perjury statute.[14] In turn the government immediately refiled perjury charges under a different law and then quickly expanded its offensive by filing charges of conspiracy and racketeering against Arnaout in October 2002. Attorney General Ashcroft said that "funds were being used to support Al Qaeda and other groups engaged in armed violence overseas" and alleged that Arnaout had funneled weapons to Al Qaeda in the late 1980s and early 1990s under bin Laden's direction. Benevolence continued to deny the charges.[15] The refiled charges, against Arnaout as an individual rather than against Benevolence as a charitable institution, gave some Muslim charitable and public policy leaders a degree of optimism that the government would target individuals rather than entire charities, despite the effects on Muslim giving in the United States.[16]

In February 2003, the government announced a plea agreement with Arnaout under which Arnaout admitted channeling charitable donations to pay for military supplies for rebels in Bosnia and Chechnya but did not admit ties to Al Qaeda. The government dropped other charges of financing terrorism, reportedly concerned that much of its case would be difficult to prove.[17] Six months later, Arnaout was sentenced to eleven years in prison for racketeering and defrauding donors. And, completing the circle on Benevolence, in November 2003, the Treasury defrocked Benevolence as a charitable organization by formally revoking its tax-exempt status.[18]

Global Relief Foundation

The Global Relief Foundation, an Islamic charity based outside Chicago that worked in a number of Muslim and non-Muslim countries, was one of thirty charitable groups investigated for links to terrorism by U.S. authorities in the 1990s.[19] The investigation of Global Relief expanded and intensified immediately after September 11, and Global Relief responded with lawsuits against several newspapers and the government. In December 2001 the government raided Global Relief's Illinois offices and froze the foundation's assets, alleging financial ties to Al Qaeda and other terrorist groups overseas, and authorities arrested a founder and board member of the foundation, Rabih Haddad, in Ann Arbor, Michigan, on immigration charges.[20] Haddad was held in solitary confinement in Chicago for four months and then moved into the prison population after dozens of complaints from supporters and a visit from his congressman, John Conyers.[21]

Haddad's arrest led to one of the first rulings against the government's attempt to keep immigration hearings on post–September 11 arrestees closed to the public and the press. The nation's chief immigration judge, Michael Creppy, had instructed immigration judges to keep post–September 11 "special interest cases" secret, ordering that "each of these cases is to be heard separately from all other cases on the docket. The courtroom must be closed . . . —no visitors, no family, and no press. This restriction includes confirming or denying whether such a case is on the docket."[22] In April 2002, a federal judge in Detroit ruled that the government could not close Haddad's immigration hearing based on the Creppy directive and that transcripts and documents from earlier secret hearings should be released. Judge Nancy Edmunds wrote that "openness is necessary for the public to maintain confidence in the value and soundness of the government's actions, as secrecy only breeds suspicion," refusing to affirm government secrecy on the detainees under the Patriot Act.[23] The Haddad case against closed hearings brought local media—particularly the *Detroit Free Press* and the *Detroit News*—together with the American Civil Liberties Union (ACLU) to oppose the Creppy directive and the government's attempts to close Haddad's and other hearings.

Two weeks later, as skirmishing between the government

and the press/civil liberties alliance continued, a federal appeals court upheld Judge Edmunds's ruling opening the Haddad hearings and documents. The same day, in a response to the Michigan and New Jersey cases, the commissioner of the Immigration and Naturalization Service instructed state and local officials to refuse to release information on immigration detainees. Faced with judicial opposition, the government relented in Haddad's case. Some of Haddad's transcripts were released, and the government stated that "the release of past transcripts," with appropriate deletions, "will not cause irreparable harm to the national security."[24]

The appeals court's formal and unanimous ruling in the Haddad case, released in late April 2002, took the government to task: "Democracies die behind closed doors. . . . When the government begins closing doors, it selectively controls information rightfully belonging to the people. Selective information is misinformation." The court also endorsed the role of the press, noting that the public regards the press as "the guardians of their liberty." And the court directly criticized Creppy's blanket secrecy directive: "The task of designating a case special interest is performed in secret, without any established standards or procedures, and the process is, thus, not subject to any sort of review. A government operating in the shadow of secrecy stands in complete opposition to the society envisioned by the framers of our Constitution."[25]

The appeals court noted that the government could attempt to close specific cases—though not as a blanket policy—if it could show a potential for physical danger, compromising investigations, or other "compelling interests sufficient to justify closure." Neither the ACLU nor the media had argued for a blanket opening of these hearings without the possibility for closure, enabling the court to reassert its traditional role. The appeals court's ruling, one of the first September 11–related cases to go against the government, was hailed by press, civil liberties groups, and other organizations around the country.[26]

Global Relief did not fare as well in its appeal to the courts to open the "secret evidence" used by the government against it under the Patriot Act.[27] Continuing to maintain his innocence, Haddad was denied political asylum in November 2002.[28] He was deported to Lebanon in July 2003.[29] His wife and children, all also ordered deported (except for one child born in the United States and therefore an American citizen), were put on a plane for Beirut in July 2003, ending the American side of the case of Rabih Haddad.[30] Global Relief's tax-exempt status was formally revoked by the Treasury in November 2003,[31] and investigations of Global Relief's ties to terrorist organizations continued.[32]

Holy Land Foundation for Relief & Development

Holy Land Foundation may well hold the dubious distinction of being the Islamic charity that has been under U.S. government scrutiny for the longest time. Holy Land was founded in the early 1990s as the Occupied Land Fund, when it was more explicit in its calls for jihad.[33] Occupied Land then moved from California to Texas, changed its name to the Holy Land Foundation for Relief and Development, ended appeals for funds for jihad, and began a rapid rise to become among the largest Muslim charities in the United States. By 2001, the last year for which the foundation's information returns are available, Holy Land had raised $13 million for what it termed charitable activities in the West Bank, Gaza, Turkey, Lebanon, Chechnya, and elsewhere in the Muslim world.

Federal investigations of Holy Land began at least as early as 1993, focusing on an alleged flow of funds to Hamas and other terrorist organizations as well as for charity in Palestinian territories. Israel refused to allow the foundation and four other groups to continue activities in 1997, calling Holy Land a "front for Hamas." And in 2000, the State Department called Holy Land a conduit for Hamas.[34]

New York and Texas attorneys general also opened highly publicized investigations of Holy Land in 2000 and 2001, and a civil suit was filed against Holy Land and other groups by the parents of an Israeli American student who had been killed in a Jerusalem terrorist attack.[35] By that time, Holy Land was raising money through a sophisticated fund-raising structure and disbursing funds in the West Bank, Gaza, Turkey, Chechnya, Kosovo, Jordan, Lebanon, and elsewhere. According to the *New York Times,* it also "contributed to food pantries in New Jersey and Texas and established a fund for the victims of the terrorist attacks on the World Trade Center and the Pentagon."[36] It had a high powered board of directors and powerful supporters in the Muslim community and was represented by lawyers at Akin, Gump, Strauss, Hauer and Feld, one of Washington's most well-connected law firms.

September 11 changed the balance in this struggle between Holy Land and federal and state authorities. In December 2001, President Bush froze almost $2 million of Holy Land's assets, alleging that it had funneled contributions to Hamas for the families of suicide bombers and other Hamas military and political activities as well as using monies for charity, and he effectively closed the foundation's Texas and New Jersey offices by having most files, computers, and other equipment seized.[37] The president's announcement focused on support for Hamas, not on Al Qaeda, September 11, Afghanistan, or Iraq, and was met by sharp opposition from Holy Land and other Muslim organizations. Some of that anger focused on the timing of the government's announcements, which were made during Ramadan, when Muslim contributions to charity are particularly high. Muslim organizations feared that the government was seeking to reduce Muslim charitable giving or at least that the timing of the announcement would have that effect.[38]

In the wake of the government's actions, several charitable gift funds that funnel contributions from individual donors to charitable organizations declined to channel additional funds to over ten Muslim charities identified in government or press reports as possibly tied to terrorist activities. The organizations acting included the Fidelity Charitable Gift Fund, the largest such organization in the United States, as well as similar funds operated by Vanguard and Charles Schwab.[39] And the powerful Akin, Gump law firm, which represented Holy Land when it was the country's largest Muslim charity with powerful supporters, dropped the foundation as a client after the president's accusations.[40]

Holy Land tried to fight back, suing the Justice, State, and Treasury Departments in March 2002 and alleging violation of its constitutional rights to free speech and religion.[41] In June 2003, a federal court upheld the government's freezing of Holy Land's assets, dismissing the foundation's free speech and free association claims and affirming that the government had substantial evidence for its determination with respect to Holy Land.[42] As with Benevolence and Global Relief, the government formally revoked the tax-exempt designation of Holy Land in late 2003.[43]

The Nonprofit Response to the Investigations & Freezing of the Muslim Charities

Actually defending Holy Land, Global Relief, and Benevolence was never a feasible strategy for the powerful American nonprofit sector. The government's offensive against those organizations and their leaders was pursued with a vigor that convinced many in the nonprofit sector that the government's actions were based solidly on evidence rather than grounded in rumor and retribution. Later, of course, it would emerge that some of the charges against the three Muslim charities were reduced, dismissed, or pursued primarily against individuals rather than against the organizations. But in the heat of the post–September 11 environment, defending Treasury-designated 501(c)(3) public charities of Muslim background that admittedly distributed funds in the Muslim world, and admittedly in some cases to terrorist organizations and the families of suicide bombers, was not considered an option by the American nonprofit sector.

Some tried to raise issues. Key Muslim organizations warned that the government's actions and rhetoric were contributing to an anti-Muslim backlash; to a sharp decline in Muslim and other contributions to recognized, organized charities; and to marginalization of Muslims. Muslim organizations pointed convincingly to a chilling in charitable donations, nonprofit activity, and public policy debate within their communities and by American Muslims in American society.[44] But outside the Muslim nonprofit and public affairs community, there were few dissenting voices. One was Richard Moyers, executive director of the Ohio Association of Nonprofit Organizations. Moyers stepped forward in the *Chronicle of Philanthropy* in October 2002 to warn of the "implications of the unprecedented effort by federal agencies, working in concert, to shut down significant charities, seize their records and assets, and force the organizations to suspend operations until their innocence can be proven." He noted that "little information has been released to substantiate" the allegations against Holy Land and that the government's allegations were based on evidence that the government refused to release to the public and even to the charities' lawyers.[45]

Instead, much of the American nonprofit community seemed to hope that an unspoken bargain—never articulated by the Justice or Treasury Departments—would control this process, a bargain that involved substantial trust in the government by the nonprofit sector. Government criminal enforcement would be limited to Muslim charities that had funneled donations to some combination of terrorist and charitable activities abroad, while the broader American nonprofit sector would remain largely unaffected by heightened government scrutiny. Moyers challenged those assumptions and that unarticulated bargain. "Will any organization be subject to the same treatment if the government claims links to terrorism? How broadly will terrorism be defined . . . ? What about eco-terrorism, or domestic disruptions such as the protests organized against global trade and financial institutions? If a major U.S. philanthropic institution is discovered to have made a grant to an organization that the government claims is linked to terrorism, will it be subject to the same 'seize and shut-down treatment'?"[46] Obviously the non-Muslim nonprofit sector did not think so, because it did not appear particularly concerned about the treatment of the Muslim charitable groups. And, of course, the environment was unfriendly to that sort of principled skepticism. "The organizations in question may indeed have supported terrorist groups, either unwittingly or intentionally. Trust in government remains relatively high, the United States is awash in patriotism, and no individual or organization wants to be perceived as supporting terrorism."[47]

In March 2002, the government expanded action against Islamic charitable organizations that it said were suspected of funneling funds to terrorist groups, including Hamas, Palestinian Islamic Jihad, and Al Qaeda. The March 2002 raids focused on a range of organizations, many headquartered in or with close links to 555 Grove Street in Herndon, Virginia, home of a number of Islamic charities and Muslim offices. A number of those organizations—among them the Muslim World League, International Islamic Relief Organization, Safa Trust, SAAR Foundation, International Institute of Islamic Thought, and others—were reportedly financed by Saudi government organizations or wealthy Saudi individuals.[48] Other actions included the indictment of four leaders of another Muslim charity, the Syracuse-based Help the Needy, that allegedly laundered money through Jordan and sent it on to Iraq.[49] And in May 2003, federal authorities froze the assets of Al Aksa International Foundation, a U.S.-based group accused of supporting Hamas, and designated it as an institutional supporter of terrorism. The U.S. action was coordinated with government raids and asset freeze orders in the United Kingdom, Denmark, and Germany.[50]

The Broader Implications of the Holy Land, Benevolence, & Global Relief Cases

Benevolence, Holy Land, and Global Relief may well have channeled charitable funds to terrorists and terrorist organizations. But there is something disturbing, even unseemly, about the reaction of the broader American philanthropic and nonprofit communities to the investigations, government statements, and indictments. As long as the investigations and indictments stayed within the Muslim charitable sector, non-Muslim organizations seemed content to remain above the fray. They did not question the accuracy or validity of the statements made about the three Muslim charities and other such groups, nor does it seem that they have ever asked when the notion of channeling funds to terrorists might be used against them as well.

Other matters should disturb the broader American philanthropic and nonprofit sector as well. There is mounting evidence of declines, perhaps substantial declines, in donations to Muslim charities in the United States and abroad. This occurred during the 2001 Ramadan season, when the government announced the freezing of assets of the Muslim charities, but there is increasing evidence of a more general reluctance to give in the Muslim community now that the community's philanthropic and nonprofit institutions are under scrutiny.[51] A more complex shift is also under way, it appears: the Muslim charities pursued by the government represented the emergence of more modern giving practices in the American community—to philanthropies and nonprofits with structures, boards, and policies; filing annual tax returns and annual reports; granted tax-exempt status by the U.S. Treasury. It may now be that the attacks on these more "modern" institutions are driving some giving in the American Muslim community back in traditional directions—by hand, in cash, directly to mosques and imams rather than to the new professional organizations. That return to tradition is unlikely to have been the government's intent, but it may well be occurring.[52]

Beyond Terrorism Financing
The Patriot Act & the Nonprofit Sector

In addition to the closing of the three Muslim charities, the freezing of their funds, and investigations of a number of other groups alleged to be involved in terrorist financing, the broader provisions of the Patriot Act and other post–September 11 laws have also had an impact on the American nonprofit sector. Of these measures, the most controversial have been Treasury Department guidelines issued in November 2002 that regulate the provision of funds by American public charities to organizations abroad. But the Patriot Act and other legal documents have also had some impact on the nonprofit sector.

The Patriot Act, for example, expanded the federal government's access to education records and enabled the government to implement a program to collect detailed information on foreign students in the United States. It also granted the government (through the Federal Trade Commission) greater freedom to regulate telemarketing, strengthened requirements that telemarketers inform call recipients of their status, and expanded the definitions of telemarketing fraud—all to respond to a sense that telemarketing fraud, using charitable fronts, might expand in the post–September 11 era as American giving for September 11 relief expanded.

Most of the more general provisions of the Patriot Act— definitions of domestic terrorism that might include nonprofits like Greenpeace or Operation Rescue, eased surveillance requirements, secret searches, and other measures—apply to or could be applied to nonprofits as well. And of course the Patriot Act, in section 806, expanded the ability of the government to seize assets of "persons engaged in planning or perpetrating . . . terrorism," or "acquired or maintained" for that purpose, or "derived from [or] involved in" terrorism. These and other measures were used, seemingly with good reason, against Holy Land, Benevolence, and Global Relief and perhaps against other nonprofits as well. They remain on the books, usable against nonprofits and charitable institutions into the future. In what appeared initially to be an innocuous provision, the Patriot Act also barred "expert advice or assistance" to designated terrorist organizations; that provision and its ramifications for American nonprofit organizations would shortly be tested in litigation.[53]

Beyond Muslim Charities
The Broadened Offensive on Overseas Funding

But, truth be told, none of this really disturbed the American nonprofit and philanthropic sector—not the investigations and indictments and broad statements about registered Muslim charities, not the possibility that the new Patriot Act could be applied energetically to the nonprofit sector well beyond a handful of Muslim charities. The nonprofit community responded to human, social, and economic needs after September 11 but failed to respond to the political dangers that September 11 also represented to itself. It was only when the government took steps that might directly affect and threaten the autonomy of an important portion of the non-Muslim American philanthropic and nonprofit sector that the sector was bestirred to a response.

That area was funding overseas by American public charities (such as Oxfam, Save the Children, and CARE) and private foundations (such as the Ford, Rockefeller, Asia, Gates, and MacArthur Foundations). The government's concern for overseas funding, and its increased scrutiny in this area, has roots in the investigations of the Muslim charities before and after September 11. It also has roots in an explicit policy of more closely scrutinizing domestic organizations that provide relief, especially to terror victims, after September 11, part of an attempt to combat fraud in the process of distributing the influx of charitable contributions made after the 2001 attacks.[54]

Before September 2001, there were laws and regulations in effect to block funds raised for charity in the United States from being used to support terrorist activities abroad, including a law blocking material support for terrorists. But these measures were substantially tightened in three separate waves after the September 11 attacks. In October 2001, the president released an executive order that expanded and made somewhat easier the freezing of assets of a range of terrorist organizations and their financiers.[55] The Patriot Act, adopted in late October 2001, further expanded the government's prerogatives in blocking terrorist financing by charitable organizations. Among other provisions, the Patriot Act broadly prohibited any provision of "expert advice or assistance" to designated terrorist organizations, including supplying of advice or assistance by American nonprofit organizations. The Humanitarian Law Project, a nonprofit that provides what it calls "human rights" information to a designated terrorist organization, the Kurdistan Workers' Party in Turkey, challenged that prohibition as overly broad and ill defined. After the Ninth Circuit Court of Appeals held that "personnel" and "training" were unconstitutionally vague in the context of "material support" in January 2004, a federal judge in Los Angeles struck down that provision of the Patriot Act as unconstitutional, saying that it "could be construed to include unequivocally pure speech and advocacy protected by the First Amendment" and "places no limitations on the type of expert advice and assistance which is prohibited." The Justice Department immediately announced that it would appeal,[56] then filed a petition for releasing in the Ninth Circuit.[57]

But it was the release of a short, seemingly innocuous seven-page document in November 2002 that finally, belatedly, began to galvanize the American nonprofit and philanthropic sector. That November, the Treasury Department's Office of Foreign Assets Control issued the *Anti-Terrorist Financing Guidelines: Voluntary Best Practices for U.S.-Based Charities,* "voluntary guidelines" on overseas giving by U.S.-based charitable organizations that prescribe "voluntary" compliance with a broad and detailed range of new provisions for charitable and philanthropic organizations.[58] No longer was the problem limited to a few Muslim charities—now the government was, in the view of some powerful nonprofits and foundations and their Washington representatives, seeking to impose new and detailed rules on how American organizations should give for relief, charity, and development overseas, under the guise of "voluntary guidelines."

The government's November 2002 "voluntary guidelines" have at least rhetorical roots in an offer made by Muslim charities as early as 1999. In 1999 and in a meeting with President Bush after the September 11 attacks, Muslim charitable and community leaders "offered the administration a proposal that would both enable the government to get the information it needs to fight terrorism and make it possible for Muslims to fulfill their religious duty . . . guidelines that Islamic charities would follow to remain free from accusations involving terrorism. The proposal centers on transparency. Muslim charities are willing to adopt a policy of complete transparency. They are eager to show the government where their money comes from and what they use it for. But to do this, they need federally sanctioned guidelines. The Treasury Department needs to spell out precisely what information it wants in order to conduct a thorough legal and financial audit, one that will provide a clean bill of health. American Muslim charities devote most of their resources to helping Muslim refugees around the world. The administration must tell us how to carry out this mission while adhering to anti-terrorism standards."[59]

The "voluntary guidelines" purport to guide American foundations, grant making charities, and individuals in donating to organizations that may in turn knowingly or unknowingly support organizations linked to terrorism. They advise that American nonprofits and foundations making grants overseas should collect considerably more information about grantees than is sometimes available, vet grantees, and review their financial operations, each in quite detailed terms.

The language of these guidelines is often exceptionally broad, and their implications have only now begun to be explored.[60] Yet their implications are crucially important. In the words of an astute policy commentator on these issues, the steps taken since 2001 carry the danger of "setting potentially unachievable due diligence requirements for international grant-making, [and] subjecting international grant-makers to high but largely undefined levels of legal risk, [which] could have the effect of reducing the already low level of legitimate international grant-making."[61]

These initiatives—particularly the Treasury Department's "voluntary guidelines"—have raised a number of important issues for the American nonprofit and philanthropic community. They include the following.

- The extent of donor liability for gifts to unnamed individuals or for benefit of unknown recipients (such as relief and disaster funds) that may, without knowledge by American organizations, also benefit terror-related organizations
- The definitions of terror-related organizations and individuals and the difficulties in determining the extent of responsibility for ascertaining any terror-related links of recipient individuals and organizations
- The extent of information gathering about recipient organizations and individuals required—quite extensive under the "voluntary guidelines"—and the difficulties in obtaining that information, as well as the conflicts with existing federal and state law that the new documents present
- The due diligence required of organizational or individual donors, which appears to exceed that required by current federal and state law
- The problems of transparency and accountability encountered by American philanthropic and charitable groups working abroad, long accustomed to a sharp separation from American diplomatic and intelligence institutions, which do not wish to be perceived by foreign organizations and governments as reporting on their overseas partners

Faced with increasing opposition from American foundations and public charities that donate abroad, in 2003 the Treasury Department requested and received extensive comments from nonprofits about the "voluntary guidelines." The nonprofit community does not appear to expect that the guidelines will be extensively revised, but clearly the groundswell of concern has put the government on notice that a powerful component of the American nonprofit sector is now concerned about government regulation in the post–September 11 environment.[62]

The British Approach Keeping Charity Regulators Central

The American approach to shutting off terrorist financing by registered charities appears largely to sidestep charity regulators rather than relying on them as partners in the antiterrorist enterprise. That approach is not the only possible means of attack on this issue. In Britain, where charities have also been used to funnel funds to external terrorist groups, the government moved quickly after September 11 to enforce the U.N. resolutions that called for freezing funds held by Al Qaeda, Taliban, and other terrorist groups. The Anti-Terrorism, Crime and Security Act of 2001 strengthened law enforcement's authority to freeze charitable and other funds bound for terrorist organizations, at the cost of controversy discussed more fully in chapter 6.

One key difference between the American and the British approaches is that in the United States the normal charity regulators—well-informed specialists in the U.S. Treasury Department's Exempt Organizations Division—appear to be somewhat marginalized in the enforcement of laws against terrorist charity financing in the United States, in favor of government units enforcing foreign assets and terrorism laws. In

England and Wales, they appear considerably more central to the process of terrorist financing enforcement.

In Great Britain, the key charity regulator is the Charity Commission, and the commission appears to have been near the forefront of charity-related terrorism financing investigations since September 11. Other investigatory and enforcement organizations have been involved, to be sure, including the National Terrorist Financial Investigation Unit (part of the Metropolitan Police), the Home Office, and numerous other security organizations. But the Charity Commission appears central to this work and has been a key public figure in enforcement, education, and explanation. In late 2001, for example, the commission initiated an investigation of the International Islamic Relief Organization after a *Times of London* report that "the charity was under CIA scrutiny in connection with the possible transfer of funds which may have been used to support the terrorist attacks in the USA." That inquiry was closed a month later after the commission found "clear evidence that the charity had ceased to operate" in Great Britain and removed it from the Central Register of Charities.[63]

The Charity Commission seems to have been careful to safeguard its role in the enforcement of charity-related terrorism financing laws in Britain, cognizant of the potential dangers to the sector and to wider charity governance when these matters are taken over wholesale by terrorism hunters and investigators. So it was not surprising when the chief officer of the Charity Commission, John Stoker, wrote of the commission's central role in early 2002. Addressing a group of readers of the liberal *Guardian* newspaper almost certainly ready to be suspicious of terrorism hunters, Stoker wrote that "[i]t's difficult to imagine an issue that could undermine public faith in British charity more than the suspicion of terrorist links." He continued firmly: "Any kind of terrorist connection is obviously completely unacceptable [and] investigating possible links with terrorism is an obvious top priority for the charity commission."[64] Having established the commission's central role in these investigations, Stoker also sought to assuage fears of a witch-hunt: "The good news is that, in both absolute and relative terms, the number of charities potentially involved are small. Neither the charity commission, nor other regulatory and enforcement organisations have evidence to suggest that the 185,000 charities in England and Wales are widely subject to terrorist infiltration."[65]

The Charity Commission's important role continued into 2002 and 2003. In May 2002, the commission reported that it had "evaluated concerns" about ten charities since the September 11 attacks and had "opened formal inquiries" into five. Of those five, two were shuttered, and the assets of one were frozen. "Vigilance is everything," warned the commission, but then it also emphasized that its relationship with the sector it regulates was useful to all. "[T]he Charity Commission is committed to working with the sector it regulates—to ensure that terror groups are never allowed to gain a foothold within England and Wales' 185,000 registered charities."[66]

That policy was detailed in "operational guidance" on "charities and terrorism" in January 2003 that reaffirmed the commission's central role in the investigation and enforcement of policies against terrorist financing. The 2003 operational guidance also reconfirmed the close relationship between the commission—through its Intelligence and Special Projects Team (ISPT)—and other intelligence, security, and law enforcement organizations.[67] In the spring of 2003, the commission issued guidelines for British charities working abroad that compare favorably to the guidelines issued to U.S. charities by the Office of Foreign Assets Control in the Treasury Department—the English guidelines focus on a risk-based approach, provide useful assistance, do not go so far in imposing new burdens on charities, and keep the process of seeking to ensure that charitable funds do not reach terrorist organizations firmly within the Charity Commission's regulatory and advisory scope.[68] Throughout all this work a recurring theme—not often loudly stated, but present—was the notion that the commission must remain at the forefront of work against terrorist financing, retaining the trust of the voluntary sector while combating terrorism, rather than cede that work to security and police organizations. As the commission's annual report for 2002 and 2003 put it, the goal is "maintaining our independence and working with others."

The central role of the commission stretched into 2003, as the commission continued a lengthy and controversial inquiry into the North London Central Mosque (Finbury Park Mosque) and an anti-American religious leader there, Sheikh Abu Hamza al-Masri. This complex case involved disputes among trustees, and allegations that Abu Hamza had "taken over" the mosque and was using it for political purposes predated September 11. But after the attacks, the commission renewed its investigation upon receiving tapes of Abu Hamza sermons that were "of such an extreme and political nature as to conflict with the charitable status of the Mosque" and investigatory reports of a "highly inflammatory and political conference" at the mosque on the first anniversary of the World Trade Center attacks. With the support of the mosque's original trustees, the commission suspended Abu Hamza from his position within the mosque, froze the mosque's accounts controlled by Abu Hamza, and in February 2003 removed him from all positions with the mosque. As part of the same inquiry, the Metropolitan Police secured the mosque and handed it back to the original trustees.[69] In late May 2004, Attorney General Ashcroft unsealed an eleven-count indictment against Abu Hamza for conspiracy to provide material support for terrorists, assistance to a 1998 bombing in Yemen, and other offenses. The British authorities promptly arrested Abu Hamza at the request of the U.S government and prepared to extradite him to the United States.

Not all commission investigations had such dramatic outcomes as the Finbury Park Mosque case. A 2002 inquiry into the Society for the Revival of Islamic Heritage was prompted by notice that the U.S. Treasury Department had issued a blocking order against a group with a similar name and offices in Pakistan and Afghanistan and that the U.S. government believed that the group "may have financed and facilitated the activities of terrorists . . . through Usama Bin Laden."[70] After investigating possible connections between the organization registered in London and the organization blocked by the U.S. government, the commission found no evidence linking the U.K. charity with the group named by the U.S. government and closed its inquiry. Another inquiry was launched in 2002 after allegations that the London-based Minhaj-Ul-Quran UK was "supporting political activities in Pakistan, record keeping at the Charity was poor and financial controls weak." After an investigation, the charity was cleared of the political support charges, and accounting controls were strengthened.[71]

The result, it appears, is considerably less suspicion of the enforcement of charity financing of terrorism in England and Wales, where a significant portion of charity finance investigations is being performed by the Charity Commission—an organization that, despite all its shortcomings, the British voluntary sector knows well and can engage in dialogue with.

Conclusion

The government's focus on curbing terrorist financing is understandable and laudable. But the nonprofit sector's failure to effectively monitor and seek improvements in the government's approaches bespeaks a relative timidity, a willingness to let certain Muslim charities fall in the hope that other parts of the sector will remain untouched. But there is gradually mounting evidence that the government's approaches, while perhaps successful in reducing some terrorist funding, are also having unfortunate effects on the levels and types of Muslim giving in the United States. And the nonprofit and philanthropic sector moved slowly into a state of concern when the Treasury Department issued "voluntary guidelines" that firmly recommend more detailed procedures for awarding funds abroad than have ever been applicable to the American nonprofit sector before. When faced with this challenge to their interests, the sector came to life, forcing at least a general reexamination of policy within the Treasury Department.

Legitimate attacks on terrorist funding have the potential to create an environment in which a considerably broader range of nonprofit and philanthropic organizations comes under fire—sometimes appropriately, sometimes not—for its activities. Hundreds of nonprofits have rallied to oppose a rule proposed by the Federal Election Commission that would make it more difficult for nonprofits to express their views on matters of public policy. The general counsel to the conservative James Madison Center for Free Speech told the *Chronicle of Philanthropy*, "The danger is that the FEC, through fiat, is going to apply the restrictions on fund-raising by political parties to all other advocacy groups. There would be no way for anyone to do grass-roots lobbying, and access to a tremendous amount of information about what Congress does would be shut off."[72]

In the fall of 2003, for example, more than a dozen members of Congress led by Representative Jerrold Nadler of New York signed a letter to the president of the Ford Foundation, demanding that the foundation take action against Ford grantees in the Middle East, primarily Palestinian groups, who have engaged in anti-Semitic or pro-terrorist statements or advocate violence or challenge the legitimacy of the state of Israel. After initial ham-handed communications efforts by the foundation, and the threat of an investigation by the Senate Finance Committee, the Ford Foundation agreed to a series of reforms and audits in its grant making and accounting procedures, terminated funding to at least one Palestinian grantee, and expressed regret for any such behavior by the foundation's grantees and gratitude to its critics.[73]

The foundation also decided to require that all Ford grantees in the United States and around the world sign new language in the foundation's standard grant acceptance agreement "requiring the organization to agree that it will not promote violence or terrorism." Those revised letters went out beginning in the fall of 2003, including to U.S. universities receiving foundation funds. The foundation's letter asked grantee institutions to agree that they will not "promote or engage in violence, terrorism, bigotry or the destruction of any state" or "make sub-grants to any entity that engages in these activities." A similar change in policy at the Rockefeller Foundation required grantees to agree that they will "not directly or indirectly engage in, promote or support other organizations or individuals who engage in or promote terrorist activity."

The foundations' new position—in effect, asking grantees to guarantee that their organizations and individuals in them would not, in the Ford Foundation wording, "promote or engage in violence, terrorism, bigotry or the destruction of any state"—prompted a swift response from nine major universities. In April 2004, the provosts of the University of Chicago, Harvard, MIT, Princeton, Stanford, Yale, and three other schools wrote to Ford and Rockefeller opposing the transfer of this burden to grantee institutions, calling the grant language vague, and warning that it might impinge on political speech. "Whatever university administrators may think of the merits of the political views expressed, these fall under the protection of freedom of academic speech," the provosts wrote. And at least two universities declined to execute the new, broad grant contract language. In the early summer of 2004, neither the foundations nor the universities seemed eager to engage in public struggle over this issue; both sides indicated that amicable discussions were continuing on the grant agreement language.[74]

But the broader implications are troubling. In the Ford case, heightened oversight by the press and legislators helped a prominent American philanthropy improve its practices. But it also came at some cost: In the current environment, there is a danger that such criticism may lead to an atmosphere that chills innovative nonprofit activity—for example, by discouraging more daring, even controversial philanthropic activity. The foundations' response has been, at least in part, to shift the burdens to the grantee institutions—universities among them—by imposing potentially broad prohibitions on conduct by faculty and others. Rather than bowing too quickly and too low to political pressure, philanthropic and nonprofit institutions must take care to admit and correct mistakes where they occurred—as did Ford when disgraceful grantee actions and statements were publicized. Yet they must also seek, openly and defiantly if necessary, to maintain the spirit of freedom, autonomy, and innovation that is the hallmark of American philanthropy and nonprofit activity.

5

Balancing Openness & Security
The State & the Academic Community
after September 11

Antiterrorism law and policy after September 11 has had contradictory effects on the academic world in the United States. Some of the worst fears of the intellectual community have not been realized—extensive and frequent searches of academic offices, extensive overt official and unofficial prejudice against Arab and Muslim intellectuals, government forays into libraries to determine what students and teachers have been reading, or government-sponsored chilling of academic and political debate.

But other effects have been clearly visible and in some cases quite serious. Surveillance of activist students and faculty seems to have increased, including recent cases in which an exceptionally wide-ranging subpoena was issued to a university to gather information on antiwar activities and army intelligence agents walked the halls of the University of Texas Law School seeking the names of students and other participants in an open academic conference. Post–September 11 restrictions and checks on visa issuance to foreign scholars and graduate students have reduced the number of students entering from certain countries and regions—especially the Middle East, China, Russia, and South Asia—while causing delays for many others. In some cases these refusals and delays have directly affected the progress and staffing of scientific and other academic work in the United States.[1]

In its concern with preventing weapons, environmental, and other information useful to terrorists from becoming available, the government has toughened secrecy rules, classified and reclassified thousands of documents, and expanded the use of new categories of government secrecy—"sensitive but unclassified" and "sensitive homeland security information"—that have provoked skepticism in both academic and civil liberties communities.[2] The government, particularly the Department of Defense and other defense- and aviation-related agencies, has also increased the use of classified research. In some cases the government has also attempted to restrict the publication of research results, require prepublication government review, or limit engagement by foreign graduate students and scholars in unclassified but "sensitive" projects.

Balancing Openness & Security Academic Freedom & Campus Debate in the World of a Resurgent State

Academic life and campus debate remained a divided picture in the post–September 11 world of American universities. As an excellent report from the American Association of University Professors indicates, academic and political debate in the United States—including debates about and criticisms of American foreign policy and, during 2003, a flaring of antiwar activities on some campuses—remain vigorous. At the same time, antiterrorism policy has also been used to chill debate and dissent.[3]

In early 2004, however, several incidents occurred in rapid succession that raised substantial concerns that the federal government has returned to using tactics unseen in decades by seeking political information about academics and students. On two campuses in different parts of the country, the government used its subpoena power and army personnel to try to identify university students and faculty interested in academic and political discussion and to quell debate.

On February 4, 2004, a federal prosecutor in Des Moines, Iowa, issued perhaps the broadest subpoena seeking political information to an American university in five decades. The order, delivered by a federal Joint Terrorism Task Force, required that Drake University hand over "all documents or recordings which would identify persons" attending a conference against American intervention in Iraq at Drake in the fall of 2003.

The subpoena also required production of all records relating to a Drake law student group, the local chapter of the National Lawyers Guild, that hosted the conference. And it sought directly to deputize university public safety officers in the federal investigation of citizens' political discussions, requiring "all records of Drake University campus security reflecting any observations" of the meeting, including "records of persons in charge" and "records of attendees."[4] The subpoena appears to have been related to a grand jury investigation of an antiwar demonstration in November at the Iowa National Guard headquarters outside Des Moines, where twelve protestors were arrested. The Joint Terrorism Task Force also subpoenaed four individuals from the Iowa Peace Network, Catholic Peace Ministry, and other antiwar groups.

In an even more chilling development, the federal prosecutors immediately followed the subpoena against the university with a gag order, signed by a federal judge, that prohibited "any officer, director, employee, agent, or attorney" at Drake—over 850 people—from disclosing the contents or even the existence of the subpoena. And then, in a move reminiscent of the Soviet era, the federal prosecutor arranged to seal the government's application for the gag order and the gag order itself in an attempt to airbrush even its order of silence from press and public attention.[5]

Is Drake an isolated case? A few days after the subpoena was issued to Drake University, army intelligence officers went from office to office at the University of Texas Law School in Austin, Texas, seeking the roster of student, faculty, and public attendees at a February 4 conference on Islam and the law. An organizer of the meeting called the conference "apolitical"; it had focused on Islam, the law, and "the different interpretations of gender issues in Islam." Rather than calling the meeting's organizer—whose telephone number and e-mail information are listed at the top of the University of Texas Law School's web page for the conference—the army intelligence officers walked the hallways, showing badges and asking law school staff for names of attendees at an academic conference.

The army intelligence officers indicated that they were investigating "suspicious" attendees at the conference, questioning the law school's special events coordinator, law student staff members of the *Texas Journal of Women and the Law*, and staff members. The army later confirmed that the agents sent to the law school are assigned to the Intelligence and Security Command based at Fort Belvoir, Virginia, although they appeared to be stationed at Fort Hood, Texas.[6] The government's direct intrusion into arenas of academic discussion and debate clearly crosses the line from hunting terrorists to dampening domestic political discussion. But the academic community's resistance has been heartening, illustrating strategies of opposition to overly broad surveillance and investigation that, again and again, stymie federal prosecutors and administration policymakers from narrowing American freedoms.

Lawyers around the country rallied to the aid of Drake University faculty and students as word spread rapidly across the country on academic, civil liberties, antiwar, and other e-mail networks—including conservative networks concerned about resurgent government power. The federal prosecutor was forced to postpone grand jury testimony and deny any link to terrorism, despite the use of the Joint Terrorism Task Force.[7] A day later, as both of Iowa's U.S. senators weighed in angrily against Justice Department abuses,[8] the president of Drake spoke publicly in opposition to the Justice Department's tactics, a gaggle of lawyers prepared for battle with the Justice Department in federal court, and hundreds of protestors demonstrated on the courthouse steps, the federal prosecutor was forced to withdraw the subpoenas and the gag order.[9] A Quaker activist reported to his friends: "We went to Des Moines for a peace rally and protest of government action, but it turned out to be [a] celebration. By the time we got there . . . the quash had happened. . . . For the next hour many speakers pontificated on the need to be vigilant and exercise our rights to free speech. There were close to 300 people there. It was cold and windy but lots of warm feelings. We got home by 4 p.m."[10]

At Texas, staff members declined to provide a roster of conference attendees or a videotape, and a student organizer reports that the law school has been "very supportive." The reaction from students and faculty was rapid: "We certainly hope that the Army doesn't believe that attending a conference on Islamic law and women is itself ground for investigation," Texas law professor Douglas Laycock told reporters.[11] A law student questioned by the agents said: "It was outrageous. He was intimidating and was using the element of surprise to try to get information out of us." The Texas law school dean expressed concern about government investigations chilling such academic gatherings.[12] And a representative of the Texas Civil Rights Project said that the government's tactics were intended to "intimidate and scare people from using the First Amendment." In March 2004, the Army Intelligence and Security Command apologized.[13]

Bringing government legal and military authority to bear against university discussions of Islam and the war in Iraq on two campuses in a single week certainly seems to reflect a certain eagerness by the U.S. military and the Justice Department to identify those participating in free speech activities and perhaps to constrain both free discussion and free association. For universities and their students and staff, these incidents clearly illustrate the power of resistance and the strength of coalitions in opposition to government intrusion and surveillance. The Drake battle quickly moved well beyond a small student law group and antiwar protestors, drawing support from federal and state legislators, university officials, academics, and civil liberties groups around the country, including conservatives. At Texas, a law school community came together to resist military surveillance as army intelligence personnel walked the hallways demanding names. Resistance and coalition building have been the key to blunting intrusions on freedoms since September 11, and these responses to the government actions perhaps prove their crucial importance once again.

Balancing Openness & Security The Visa Debate

It is a common perception that most, if not all, of the September 11 hijackers entered the United States on student visas. That is not actually the case—one of the nineteen hijackers entered on a student visa, for a flight school rather than a university, and several more were issued student visas by a less-than-competent Immigration and Naturalization Service well after they died on September 11. But the perception remains, and a belief that potential terrorists easily can enter the United States as students and scholars appears to have pervaded the government as well. That view in turn has been fueled by the high numbers of foreign graduate students and scholars powering sophisticated American research in science and technology. In 2002, about 550,000 foreign students were studying in the United States, a rapid increase over the past several decades.[14] In 2000, the last year for which detailed data is available, foreign students constituted about 35 percent of all recipients of doctoral degrees in science and engineering in the United States and 49 percent of doctoral recipients in mathematics and computer science.[15]

The result in the wake of September 11 was clear: an evident attempt to prevent other potential terrorists from entering the United States on student, scholar, or other types of visas. The implementation of that valid goal has prevented some foreign students and scholars from pursuing education and research here; driven others to academic work in Europe, Australia, or elsewhere; and prompted a significant protest in the academic community. Hundreds, perhaps thousands, of foreign students and scholars were denied visas or merely told to wait—in some cases for months or longer while their applications were processed. A number of students and scholars already in the United States who returned home to visit family, particularly in 2001 and 2002, were unable to obtain return visas to continue their work in the United States.[16]

Occasionally lost in the attempts to screen foreign students and scholars following September 11 are the benefits these individuals bring to the United States. Higher education is the fifth largest American export in the services sector, according to the Commerce Department. And that export—though we do not usually think of education as an export—accrues at least $12 billion to the United States each year in spending by foreign students and scholars.[17] Foreign graduate students and scholars are also crucial for staffing university laboratories, and they help provide the edge that keeps American science and technology at the world's leading edge. Universities and scientists emphasize these points, and the government recognizes them, but policy implementation after September 11 has had significant and, occasionally, avoidable effects on this crucial sector for American innovation and prosperity.

Preventing Student & Scholar Terrorists
The Problems with SEVIS

In reality, government attempts to prevent potential terrorists from entering the United States as students or scholars go back many years. Following the first World Trade Center bombing in 1993, Congress mandated the establishment of a computerized database for foreign students and scholars that could track them from foreign consulate through U.S. school, including changes of location and field of study, all usable in "real time" by diplomatic, immigration, university, security, and other officials. In the world before September 11 the academic community had qualms about a system that would provide so much information to the government, including security and intelligence officials, and move such a significant record-keeping burden from the Immigration Service to individual educational institutions. But those qualms largely disappeared after the terrorist attacks—partly because some of the policy alternatives, such as a threatened moratorium on student and scholar visas, would have been far worse.

The Patriot Act revived the foreign student and scholar

tracking program, enlarged it to include flight schools and language schools, and enabled the federal government to obtain more information about foreign students and scholars and their activities and communications.[18] With funding in place, the government told universities and other educational institutions that all foreign students and scholar data needed to be entered online in the system—now renamed SEVIS, for Student and Exchange Visitor Information System—by 2003.

The problem, as might be imagined, is that the system did not work particularly well. University staff entered data, and it disappeared. Confidential student and scholar data entered in Iowa might print out in Utah. Batch files used to load or download data for hundreds of students failed to operate. SEVIS categories did not always match legal categories, requiring approvals on some issues that the law indicated were automatic. In the early stages of the SEVIS program, visa officers in U.S. embassies and consulates abroad could not access the data and thus denied visas to specific students and scholars, although universities had entered data into the system for just those individuals so that they could apply for visas. No effective provision had been made for foreign students and scholars to pay the additional fees the government considered necessary to maintain the system. Throughout the country, universities were forced to add personnel and hardware to their foreign student and scholar management systems to try, often unsuccessfully, to deal with the failures of SEVIS. The problem was complicated by the traditional bifurcation of visa authority between the State Department and the Immigration and Naturalization Service and then was exacerbated when the new Department of Homeland Security took over the Immigration and Naturalization Service, a needed but often criticized agency, in 2003.

Faced with these difficulties, the government allowed a

series of extensions and delays in the entry of data by universities and other schools. Gradually the technical and implementation issues improved, but in late 2003, the government issued regulations ordering that foreign student visa applicants pay a nonrefundable "SEVIS fee" of $100 by check, money order, or credit card. This sparked a new round of criticism, including a prominent letter to the Department of Homeland Security from the American Council on Education and twenty other education and exchange groups severely criticizing the implementation of the fee requirement.[19] And in December 2003, a joint report by the Center for Immigration Studies and NumbersUSA Education and Research Foundation found that the government had missed many of the targets for reporting accurately on foreign students and scholars mandated in the Enhanced Border Security and Visa Entry Reform Act of 2002.[20] After several years of implementation of SEVIS, the sober situation was summed up by Scott King, director of the Office of International Students and Scholars at the University of Iowa: "With the full implementation of the Student and Exchange Visitor Information System (SEVIS), and the addition of other restrictions placed on entering and staying in the U.S., we have seen a significant impact on the faculty's ability to recruit the best and brightest students."[21]

Repelling Terrorist Students & Scholars
The MANTIS & Condor Programs

SEVIS was an attempt to rationalize and toughen the student and scholar visa process, both to enable the government to get a better grasp of who was in the United States, where, studying what, and for how long; and to prevent potential terrorists from entering as foreign students or scholars. As such, it was not directly aimed at the terrorism issue. Two other new programs more directly targeted potential terrorists. Each attempted to balance America's traditional openness to foreign students and international scientific collaboration with a need to keep out some students and scholars who wished to study or use materials that might be used against the United States. As might be expected, that was and remains an exceptionally difficult balance.

Once again, the roots of these programs go back well before September 11. Under the federal immigration laws, the State Department developed a Technology Alert List (TAL) of sensitive areas of study and possible sources of illegal technology exports in the 1990s. Before and after September 11, those sensitive fields included munitions, nuclear technology, aircraft propulsion, biotechnology, cryptography and information security, and ten other technical fields. Countries of particular concern included the seven states defined as "state supporters of terrorism"—Cuba, Iran, Iraq, Libya, North Korea, Sudan, and Syria—and five states of particular concern for nuclear proliferation—China, India, Israel, Pakistan, and Russia. When visa officers identified an applicant pursuing studies in one of those sensitive science-related fields, from one of the named countries, the application was generally referred to an interagency review in Washington for further screening in a process known as MANTIS, or "science-related screening."[22]

In the summer of 2002, the State Department expanded the fields of study on the Technology Alert List subject to MANTIS to include urban planning and a range of other areas.[23] Because of both the expansion of academic fields subject to special inquiries and the increasing use of the program by visa officers, MANTIS referrals to Washington jumped from about two thousand in 2001 to about fourteen thousand in 2002. In each MANTIS case visa issuance was delayed under a policy that did not allow visa officers to issue documents until the security and intelligence organizations responding to a MAN-TIS inquiry came back with a clean "yes." Numerous factors have collided to produce substantial problems with the MAN-TIS "sensitive technology" process. Visa officers often do not have the technical background, or enough information on visa applicants, to differentiate between work on technical subjects that may have military or terrorist implications and that which furthers basic research. Visa officers may be considerably more willing, particularly in the post–September 11 environment, to refer cases to Washington in which applicants mention any TAL field whatsoever. And, of course, the TAL fields have been greatly expanded, adding the danger of overcoverage to the problems with this structure.

A separate visa screening process seeks to investigate applicants for student and scholar visas to screen out potential terrorists. Named "Visa Condor," this program also involves referrals of particular visa applicants, including applicants for business visas, from embassy-based visa officers to Washington. The Condor antiterrorist screening process also had a large backlog in 2002—of over ten thousand visa applicants—that was being reduced through the efforts of an interagency working group.[24]

Registration Requirements for Foreign Students & Scholars

In 2001, faced with dysfunctional Immigration Service databases unable to count or track foreign citizens residing in the United States on visitor, business, student, and other visas, the government ordered all males aged sixteen to forty-five from twenty mostly Arab and Muslim countries to register with the Immigration Service. This special registration program, limited to males from certain Arab and Muslim countries, sparked substantial opposition in the Arab, Muslim, and civil liberties communities, as well as in academic communities with significant numbers of students and scholars from those countries. The program ended in 2003, with little visible indication that it had resulted in terrorist interdiction, but it had clearly produced substantial fear in the Arab and Muslim communities.[25]

All of these programs have been under review by the White House and the Department of Homeland Security under a presidential order issued in October 2001. The results of that review have been delayed several times, apparently because of the problems involved in balancing these complex issues while also trying to manage a difficult and overwhelmed system. Beginning in 2004, many of the sensitive and complicated visa issues are expected to be decided by a new Interagency Panel for Advanced Sciences and Security (IPASS), intended to provide special screening for students, scholars, and scientists from certain sensitive countries studying "sensitive topics" that are "uniquely available" in the United States. IPASS is intended to improve upon the current MANTIS system, as well as to cover changes in study fields by students already in the United States.[26] Universities have only sporadically been consulted in the process, leading to increasing skepticism that the IPASS system will balance security and openness to foreign students and scientists any better than the current system.[27]

As 2003 opened, these problems were not being resolved effectively, and restrictions on established scientists were becoming a particular problem. The presidents of the National Academy of Sciences, the National Academy of Engineering, and the Institute of Medicine issued a joint statement criticizing the government's restrictiveness in granting visas to foreign scholars and scientists: "[O]ngoing research collaborations have been hampered; . . . outstanding young scientists, engineers, and health researchers have been prevented from or delayed in entering this country; . . . important international conferences have been canceled or negatively impacted. . . . Prompt action is needed."[28] Parsing the problem helped a bit. The government appeared responsive to the blunt criticisms about problems in bringing experienced scientists to the United States, for that was distinguishable from the broader issue of granting visas to foreign graduate students and younger scientists. The president's science adviser, for example, addressed that issue and the broader visa problem when he conceded to the National Academy of Sciences in June 2003 that "[t]he long delays in issuing visas to scientists and students appears to be having a significant impact on the U.S. science enterprise."[29]

The results of this confusion and conflict are not encouraging. As a nation we face several additional threats arising from the difficulty in effectively managing our visa and tracking systems for foreign students and scholars. A number of the most talented foreign graduate students and scholars may decide to go elsewhere for graduate study and research. There is an increasing set of options for foreign students and scholars because Europe, Australia, and Asia are now aggressively marketing graduate and research programs and have additional funds available to bring in such scholars and students.[30]

At root, these are problems both of management and of coverage. Certainly administration needs improvement. As the president of the Association of American Universities put it in 2002, at the height of these problems: "We need higher education, INS, and the State Department to sit down and be managerially responsible and simply have a finite, minimalist tracking system [that gives the Congress and the] public confidence."[31] And the universities strongly and correctly prefer that these hard decisions be made at the visa stage rather than when a foreign student or scientist is already in the

United States. MIT and other institutions have made it clear that their universities are open institutions, that students admitted and issued visas may take courses freely and participate in university events, academic and otherwise. If students are to be excluded on security grounds, they should be excluded at the borders. Any other sort of exclusion, such as from specific courses or programs once a student is on campus, is generally unacceptable to the universities.[32]

On the other hand, we must seek to avoid the investigation of overly broad groups, which makes it less likely that we will discover actual or potential terrorists, clogs our investigatory and tracking systems with thousands of irrelevant inquiries, and antagonizes many who seek to be our friends. And we must find administrative means of investigating potential students and scholars that do not put us at a severe competitive disadvantage vis-à-vis countries that also want the most talented graduate students and scholars to help build their science and technology sectors. All of this might argue for a system that is, in the words of the Association of International Educators, "focused and multilateral."[33] We are having substantial difficulty in focusing such a tracking and investigatory system, and at least by mid-2004 any notion of a "focused and multilateral" structure, even at the conceptual level, seemed far away.

Balancing Openness & Security The Expansion of Government Secrecy & the Scientists' Response

There is a long history of tension between government secrecy and freedom of information in American life. In the post–September 11 era, relations between the government and the academic community in the arena of government secrecy have focused on two key areas. The first is attempts by the government to expand the classification of information and by the academic community to maintain the openness of research and scientific information. Much of this conflict between government and academics is based upon the government's attempts to expand the classification of documents to include broad new categories of "sensitive but unclassified" information and "sensitive homeland security information" that are to be kept confidential although they fall outside statutory classification schemes. A second important area of conflict and negotiations is the government's sporadic but increasing attempts to review, approve, or modify university-based scientific research before publication. And the post–September 11 era has put substantial strain on the policy of many universities to avoid classified research or to consign it to dedicated, segregated facilities.

"Sensitive but Unclassified" & "Sensitive Homeland Security Information" A New Battleground

Classification of information has been an important battleground since long before September 11, but it took on increased strength after the terrorist attacks. National authorities seek to restrict dissemination of information they consider inimical to national security; intellectuals generally seek the widest possible openness in access to information. This conflict has existed since at least the days of development of nuclear technology in the 1940s. In the late 1980s and early 1990s, some semblance of a balance between governmental and academic concerns over information was achieved, reasonably successfully, through National Security Decision Directive 189 (NSDD-189), issued by President Reagan in 1985. The 1985 directive promised "no restrictions . . . upon the conduct or reporting of federally-funded fundamental research that has not received national security classification." In other words, official classification was the sole method for keeping federally funded research from the public eye, and universities could decide whether or not to accept funds with those conditions. Some universities do not accept research funds for classified projects, some do, and some (such as MIT) do so but conduct the research in separate facilities.

The Reagan era NSDD-189 approach certainly did not do away with classified government information. It generally did ensure that academics would enter a research relationship with the government reasonably clear as to what was releasable or publishable and what was not and could make their decisions accordingly. The president's national security adviser, Condoleeza Rice, reaffirmed that NSDD-189 remained the policy of the Bush administration in November 2001, also reaffirming that "open and collaborative" basic research is supported by the government.[34]

But in the post–September 11 era, the government has also identified a wide range of information that is not officially classified but that it does not want released, ostensibly out of concern that such information could be used effectively by terrorists. And, as with other post–September 11 restrictions, these policies did not begin with the bombing of the World Trade Center and the Pentagon. Over a dozen government agencies were placing restrictions on release of unclassified information, using dozens upon dozens of different terms, well before September 11. Such information includes environmental data, infrastructure information, privacy data, police and law enforcement information, and other matters.

But this process of restricting release of information that has not been classified clearly accelerated after September 11 in an atmosphere of increased government secrecy and out of a desire to prevent valuable information from being used by terrorists—though it can be hard to distinguish the latter, more laudable, antiterrorist motive from a less defensible penchant for government secrecy. With the Department of Defense in the lead, a number of government agencies have begun reclassifying significant amounts of formerly unclassified information as "sensitive but unclassified" information or "sensitive homeland security information," contrary to at least the spirit of National Security Decision Directive 189 and against the growing protests of academic figures, universities, government secrecy activists, and others. The Defense and Energy Departments and several other federal departments began reclassifying certain information into the "sensitive but unclassified" category after September 11, withdrawing some information from public view.[35]

In March 2002, the president's chief of staff, Andrew Card, released a widely cited memorandum to all government departments ordering that federal agencies throughout the government secure "sensitive but unclassified" information and "sensitive homeland security information." The changing policy was formalized in the legislation that established the Department of Homeland Security, the Homeland Security Act of 2002. The Homeland Security Act required government departments to protect both "sensitive but unclassified" and "sensitive homeland security" information, both defined broadly.[36]

The increasing use of the "sensitive but unclassified" and "sensitive homeland security" tags has had a number of implications for the research community. In some cases, federal agencies have attempted to insert contract language into federal research agreements with universities, binding universities and researchers not to release information that the government defines as "sensitive but unclassified" or "sensitive homeland security" information. Some universities have occasionally been able to avoid such requirements through negotiation.

Others have sought to resist such restrictive contract language that effectively adds a new layer of classification largely dependent on government definitions and discretion but have not been successful. And still other institutions, eager to receive federal research funding, including significant new amounts of defense and homeland security funding in an era of declining resources, have accepted federal funds without significantly questioning the new classification schema.

In addition, after Andrew Card's White House memorandum, a number of government departments began withdrawing previously open and unclassified information from government web sites and libraries. According to the American Association for the Advancement of Science, the administration "began withdrawing more than 6,500 declassified documents relating to sensitive chemical and biological warfare information from public access" in 2002. There have also been reports that the government has "order[ed] that information at public libraries be removed from public access or be destroyed" and "stopped providing information that used to be routinely released to the public."[37]

Government departments have been told to use an expanded interpretation of exemptions under the Freedom of Information Act to justify refusals to provide "sensitive but unclassified" or "sensitive homeland security" information to the public. Now, according to the Justice Department, the government will defend a government agency refusing to release information where there is a "foreseeable risk" of harm from release of the information. That is considerably broader than the earlier standard.

Finally, the government's actions and the situation since September 11 have prompted extensive discussion of self-censorship and self-regulation by the academic and research communities. Journals in microbiology and other fields have, with government encouragement, begun to put in place mechanisms to remove or limit information that conceivably might be useful to terrorists. The mechanisms vary from special reviews of sensitive papers on sensitive topics to removing the "methodology" sections of certain papers so that terrorists cannot replicate processes. A number of scientists support these efforts, both as a means to limit information that should not be accessible to potential terrorists and to avoid stricter government intervention in the research world; others think that by implementing these measures the journals have already gone too far.

Academic and research institutions and their personnel have raised a number of problems with the increasing restrictions on what the government calls "sensitive but classified" or "sensitive homeland security" information. The White House, Justice, and Homeland Security Departments have not provided clear definitions of these terms or cogent explanations of the types of materials that fall into these categories. The broad and general standards that have been described place no reasonable limit on the amount or sorts of information that could be restricted. In the fall of 2002, the government indicated that it would seek to develop workable guidelines for the definition of "sensitive but classified" and "sensitive homeland security" information, focusing on "consistent treatment among the different agenc[ies]."[38]

But leaders of the American academic and research communities continued to warn of the dangers of government categorization of unclassified information under the "sensitive" and other monikers. In October 2002, the presidents of the National Academy of Sciences, the National Academy of Engineering, and the Institute of Medicine issued a public statement noting that "[a] successful balance between . . . security and openness . . . demands distinctions between classified and unclassified research. We believe it to be essential that these distinctions not include poorly defined categories of 'sensitive but unclassified' information that do not provide precise guidance on what information should be restricted from public access. . . . [V]ague criteria of this kind generate deep uncertainties among both scientists and officials. . . . The inevitable effect is to stifle scientific creativity and to weaken national security."[39] The presidents of three major university associations, including the Association of American Universities, delivered a similar message to the White House science adviser in 2003: "New ill-defined categorizations will create severe uncertainty among researchers and adversely impact the ability of students and faculty to conduct fundamental research across many, if not all, science and engineering fields."[40]

The Expansion of "Sensitive" Government Prepublication Review of Scientific Research & Limitations on Foreign Students & Scholars

The problem of "sensitive but unclassified" and "sensitive homeland security" information has been closely related to another disturbing development for university researchers: the increasing trend among government agencies to seek to require government clearance or other control before academic researchers can publish results based upon unclassified and unrestricted research. Hewing closely to the terms of the Reagan 1985 National Security Decision Directive might help to resolve the problem. The concern is that the government is increasingly seeking to impose such controls on unclassified research, a violation of at least the spirit of the 1985 National Security Decision Directive.

Again, this problem cannot be clearly bifurcated between the era before September 11 and the difficult years since.

Before September 11, for example, highly complex export control laws also created problems for universities in determining when even unclassified research might need to be reviewed by the government before dissemination. But since September 11, government contract and grant clauses increasingly call for some form of prepublication review of research data, leading to increasing dissension at the university level and complicated contract negotiations between a number of universities and government agencies. The previously mentioned letter to the president's science adviser also addressed these issues. "These clauses," the heads of the university associations wrote, "attemp[t] to control fundamental research with the potential to move into sensitive but unclassified areas. Such contract terms create a 'gray area,' where it is difficult, if not impossible, to determine whether research is in fact controlled. The uncertainty is aggravated by the fact that the federal agency officials have not been forthcoming with explanations."[41]

Government concern for the murky area of "sensitive but unclassified" research also results in attempts to place restrictions on the individuals who can work on federally funded unclassified but "sensitive" work. In some cases since September 11, government agencies have attempted, through government contracts, to bar foreign students and researchers from certain research or to require screening of all such foreign individuals. Universities have objected to both efforts, though not consistently. Several institutions have refused significant federal funds for research because the government sought to impose such restrictions, the universities resisted, and the two sides could not come to a workable compromise. Here again, as the president of the Association of American Universities and several other university associations warned, the "gray area" of "sensitive but unclassified" research has "a pernicious effect" that threatens academic freedom.

Universities and their researchers understand full well that the balancing of openness and security will require consideration and resolution of these difficult problems. What concerns them—even causes fear—is the prospect of inflexible or overly broad regulations or other guidelines regarding prepublication approval or review; employment of foreign students or scientists; or other matters that, in the words of the heads of the university associations, "inherently compromise the openness, vitality and productivity of our university enterprise."[42] The plea here is for process, for cooperation rather than the unilateral imposition of rules drawn up by Defense, Homeland Security, or other departments that, justifiably or not, lean heavily to the side of security rather than to an effective and sophisticated balance.

There have been varying governmental responses to these objections from the academic and research community. The president's science adviser, a distinguished scientist himself, has sought to intervene with other government agencies to offer constructive "suggestions" on contract language and policy. And he has lauded the efforts in the biological community to self-govern sensitive publications.[43] From that perspective, assertive self-regulation may be used by more flexible academic organizations as a means to forestall more intrusive government regulation on issues such as publication and the employment of foreign researchers. At the same time, as might be expected in a broad array of government agencies with different interests and policies along the spectrum of security and openness, a number of defense, homeland security, space, aviation, and other agencies funding university-based research have continued to try to assert controls, either through requiring prepublication approval or review, or attempting to limit foreign involvement in research, or through other means, all outside the formal classification framework enshrined in National Security Decision Directive 189.

Balancing Openness & Security Biological Research & the Problem of "Select Agents"

A strengthened system for the registration and control of hazardous biological agents was another result of the September 11 attacks and the as yet unsolved 2001 anthrax attacks in Washington and New York. Biological research has traditionally had a quite different relationship with government than nuclear research and some other sensitive research areas. As the American Association of University Professors has put it: "[I]n the past, university research in the biological sciences has never been subject to the government's secrecy requirements; . . . university officials have opposed secret biological research; and [the key federal funder did] not support classified [biodefense] research."[44] Some of that began to change rapidly in the months after September 11.

Yet as with foreign student and government secrecy issues, there had been considerable movement on this problem before the terrorist attacks. The 1995 bombing of the Alfred P. Murrah Federal Building in Oklahoma City by American terrorists, which killed 168, helped to prompt increasing attention to the spread of these agents, although the Oklahoma City bombing did not use a biological agent. A 1996 law required the Department of Health and Human Services to identify biological agents in need of control and tracking and to register university and other facilities that transported such agents. These were, at least originally, fairly narrow requirements: organizations experimenting with rather than transporting the hazardous agents were not required to register with the government, for example, though weapon uses of such agents were barred.[45]

In due course the Centers for Disease Control (CDC) identified and published a list of "select agents" subject to registration, along with requirements that registering and transporting organizations, primarily universities, agree to CDC inspections and be able to dispose of the agents effectively. Even before September 11 and the anthrax attacks, many scientists considered this system inadequate. The rights-minded Federation of American Scientists, for example, criticized the early mechanism for its lack of any "central inventory of dangerous microbes and toxins and because many laboratories that work on anthrax are unregistered."[46]

This rather limited system came under even more sustained criticism after September 11 and the anthrax attacks. Congress focused on four issues clearly identified by the Congressional Research Service: "expanding the requirements for registration of laboratories beyond transport; identifying and registering laboratories that store and use biological agents that could be used in terrorist attacks; refining lists of toxic biological agents and monitoring their use [rather than merely transport]; and limiting access of unregistered and potentially threatening users to certain biological materials." The issues for public debate mirrored those legislative problems: access to biological agents, the burdens on universities and laboratories in any enhanced regulatory system, the scope of the agents required to be registered, and the range of institutions subject to enhanced regulation.[47]

From Underprotection to Overinclusion?

The Patriot Act fired the first new salvo in expanding and tightening American law relating to hazardous biological agents. It provided criminal sanctions for possession of biological agents beyond "prophylactic, protective, bona fide research, or other peaceful purposes" and banned certain types of individuals, including felons, illegal aliens, aliens from specific countries that support terrorism, and others, from contact with the identified biological agents. The Department of Health and Human Services was allowed to enlarge the list of regulated select agents.

No appeals or waiver procedure was provided, nor was it made entirely clear who was responsible for identifying users. The university? The government? And what kind of information would pass legal muster? These concerns were by no means trivial: the university and research community sought some sort of appeals or waiver procedure, noting that "with a waiver process in place, restricted persons who pose no security threats but are key to making research advances might still be able to contribute to searches for vaccines and cures."[48]

The original version of the act, as in a number of other areas, had been even more strict. Industry and academic lobbyists, for example, succeeded in adding the exception for "bona fide research," and an original version of the act would have barred all foreign personnel from working with select agents. Nevertheless, some of the biological agents provisions of the act still came in for criticism. For example, the "subjectivity" of the exception for "bona fide research" was questioned by many, including Senator Patrick Leahy. Leahy said that the allowance for "bona fide research" "may yet prove unworkable, unconstitutional, or both" and could "have a chilling effect upon legitimate scientific inquiry." He asked for more specific language that would "provide prosecutors with a more workable tool."[49]

Congress continued to debate bioterrorism and select agents legislation into 2002. A key issue was balancing restrictions with the openness and creativity needed for advanced science. "Implementation of restrictive controls to impede access to biological agents is inherently difficult and potentially could also deter the critical research and diagnostic activities to combat terrorism," prominent microbiologist Ronald Atlas had told the

Senate Judiciary Committee late in 2001. "Much of the material and equipment is in widespread use and commercially and internationally available; dangerous pathogens are naturally occurring; and, the research and technology knowledge base relevant to biological weapons is publicly available."[50]

Other knotty issues included the extent of exclusion of foreign graduate students and scientists from laboratories using "select agents" and how many of the potentially thousands of laboratories were to be regulated. The scope of laboratory coverage was a difficult issue because the 1996 rules had only regulated about 350 labs that engaged in transport of biological agents, not the many thousands that actually use one or more such agents. The question of enforcement was increasingly raised, for the Centers for Disease Control resisted that role and no other government agency seemed capable of taking it up.

For some universities, select agents were rapidly becoming troublesome issues as well. At the Massachusetts Institute of Technology, a high level committee noted that the Patriot Act's requirements "are not consistent with MIT's principles. It is likely that in the current climate, the number of agents on the list will grow and the restrictions placed on personnel, physical access, and publication of research findings may grow as well. At some point, MIT may rightfully decide that on-campus research in [these] areas . . . is no longer in its interest or in line with its principles." The committee urged caution and consideration of a "sunset clause" for all new government or private contracts that carried such restrictions.[51]

After months of congressional debate, in June 2002 Congress passed and the president signed the Public Health Security and Bioterrorism Preparedness and Response Act, which expanded regulation beyond transport to the users of and experimenters with biological agents. Within three months, by September 2002, all life science researchers around the country were required to report on their inventories of the forty select agents in the earlier CDC list, as well as certain other agricultural materials. An indication of the scope of the new law and the federal concern for biological agents is that the CDC sent forms to over two hundred thousand institutions requiring a response, even if the institution did not have select agents. The new law also required laboratories and other facilities holding select agents to conduct background checks on personnel with access to such materials.[52] Noncitizens from countries defined by the government as supporting terrorists continued to be banned from transporting and using biological agents, as were felons, those convicted of drug-related offenses, and several other groups. And laboratories holding select agents were required to formulate security plans for those materials.

These new requirements, while generally accepted, also prompted a national university association to note "great uncertainty" amid "conflicting advice from federal officials" about the scope of the new rules and whether select agent research would be permitted to go on.[53] The new law put immediate and substantial burdens on universities, laboratories, and researchers across the nation. In a few cases researchers, laboratories, or universities decided to dispose of stocks of biological agents rather than go through the complex process of reporting them to the government and developing security plans to protect them.[54] MIT president Charles Vest noted that "even this seemingly straightforward approach is not without a huge potential price to be paid in the advancement of science, and therefore in our health and welfare." Echoing the earlier high level university report, he stated that "we could soon arrive at a level of restriction . . . on the basis of . . . citizenship, for example—something that would be incompatible with our principles of openness, and could cause us to withdraw" from such research.[55]

A number of issues have arisen with regard to the increasing, if necessary, regulation of biological agents. In 2002 a University of Connecticut graduate student, Tomas Foral, became the first person charged with possession of a biological agent in violation of the tightened provisions of the Patriot Act, when government investigators allegedly found two undeclared specimens of anthrax in a laboratory freezer. Foral protested that he had saved them innocently after cleaning up specimens that dated back to the 1960s. His university claimed that he had been told to destroy them.[56] Public groups that track research on biological agents have been rebuffed in seeking information on research under way. In one case, the University of Texas Medical Branch in Galveston refused to provide all the information requested by a nonprofit group, the Sunshine Project, on its biodefense research and grant applications, citing federal and state law, including the need to protect "sensitive homeland security information."[57]

Information on biological agents is already widely available, and the agents themselves are readily accessible too.[58] Therefore, scientists have begun to question the actual value of broad, enhanced regulation. Restriction also has gone hand in hand with the availability of significant federal funds for research on bioterrorism; the National Institutes of Health planned to spend at least $300 million in 2003 on biodefense centers and laboratories, sparking intense competition among American universities for those facilities—and opposition in some. In Davis, California, for example, significant opposition developed to the plans of the University of California at Davis to build a biodefense laboratory with federal funds.[59]

Partly as a result of the issues arising from the rapid increase in government regulation of biological agent research, in late 2003 the National Academy of Sciences' Committee on Research Standards and Practices to Prevent the Destructive

Application of Biotechnology called for "build[ing] on existing measures within the scientific community to screen plans for certain types of experiments before they are conducted," through a government-created but independent National Science Advisory Board for Biodefense. The new board would include both scientists and security personnel from outside and within government. The authors of the recommendation called it a "key step in an evolving process to strike the right balance between security concerns and the openness necessary for America's research enterprise to thrive."[60] The report also called for international standards for appropriate biodefense research, because stricter standards in the United States make little sense at a time when such research is feasible and its results available in a number of other countries as well. At the same time, a number of scientific journals either adopted policies of "self-review" or "self-censorship"—clearly hoping to head off more significant government regulation or prepublication review—or urged their authors to do so.

6

The Resurgence of the State
Civil Liberties & the Struggle against
Terrorism in Comparative Perspective

September 11 & the Resurgence of the State

The forcefulness of response to the attacks of September 11 in law and policy was not merely an American phenomenon. Around the world we have seen a resurgence of the state, expressed through creation and implementation of antiterrorism legislation and policy in the wake of the September 11 attacks. Of course these reactions have taken different forms in various countries, but in many countries they share a basic characteristic: the state is reasserting itself, extending the reach of its powers in the name of national security and antiterrorism, and provoking varieties of opposition. Governmental responses have often been more pronounced—and perhaps more justified—in nations in which terrorist attacks of various kinds are a continuing issue rather than a new problem. This chapter discusses the resurgence of the state in antiterrorist policy in three key countries that pride themselves on their democratic heritage and principles:

- the United Kingdom, which has had a long history of terrorism and antiterrorism efforts;
- Australia, which did not have any significant history of terrorism or antiterrorism efforts but implemented new regulations after September 11; and
- India, a developing country with a long and complex tradition of antiterrorist legislation and enforcement that was vigorously reinforced after the September 11 events.

Although each of these countries responded in somewhat different ways to the September 11 events, there are certain important commonalities in their responses. First, each moved with urgency to strengthen state capacity to investigate, detain, charge, and punish a more broadly defined range of terrorist or terrorist support activities, often including aspects of domestic political dissent, through the enactment or amendment of antiterrorist legislation. In each case states sought to forestall and preempt debate and opposition through extraordinarily rapid adoption of new or strengthened laws in the postattack era.

The modes of that resurgence of state power have had certain commonalities as well: each of these countries has sought to expand the definitions of antistate (terrorist or treasonous) activities; relax requirements for detention of a broadened range of suspects; expand the availability of wiretaps and electronic surveillance; tighten restrictions on terrorist financing through charities; detain, often incommunicado, suspected terrorists or political dissidents; deport terror suspects; strengthen screening of air and other transport passengers; and increase surveillance of suspected terrorist and dissident groups. In most of these states the expansion of "terrorist" related crimes was so broad that it implied the criminalization (or recriminalization) of sedition by another name, in some cases long after the offense of sedition had been removed from the laws or substantially limited in practice.

Finally, each of these nations has followed initial legislation and enforcement with a second wave of new, even tougher, antiterrorism proposals that would further restrict privacy and broaden the reach of the state. In the calmer atmosphere of 2002 and 2003, this second wave of antiterrorism law and policy elicited stronger, broader, and better organized opposition from an expanding alliance of skeptics in Britain, Australia, and India, just as it has in the United States.[1]

The United Kingdom

The British scholar Paul Wilkinson has clearly pointed out the potential contradictions between civil liberty and antiterrorism legislation. He notes that "the primary objective of any counter-terrorist strategy must be the protection and maintenance of liberal democracy . . . [but] it cannot be sufficiently stressed that this aim overrides in importance even the objective of eliminating terrorism and political violence as such."[2] This balancing is as important in the United Kingdom as in the United States, and coming to that balance is proving to be as difficult and controversial a task across the Atlantic as in our own country.

The United Kingdom has long had more draconian antiterrorist legislation in place than the United States and other countries, largely as a result of the wars in Northern Ireland and the violence they spawned within England and other parts of the United Kingdom. Earlier antiterrorist regulations were often provisional in nature, but in many cases they were made permanent by the Terrorism Act (2000), which predated the September 11 attacks. The Terrorism Act outlawed twenty-five terrorist organizations; provided law enforcement with stop and search powers and detention authority for up to seven days; and defined new criminal offenses tied to terrorism,

including "inciting terrorist acts," "seeking or providing training for terrorist purposes at home or overseas," and "providing
instruction or training in the use of firearms, explosives or
chemical, biological or nuclear weapons."[3]

After September 11, the government of Prime Minister
Tony Blair quickly pushed through new legislation—the Anti-
Terrorism, Crime and Security Act of 2001—to expand
antiterrorism provisions and fill gaps in existing law, at least as
perceived by the government. The 2001 Anti-Terrorism Act
permitted the government to detain foreign citizens "suspected
of involvement in international terrorism but who cannot be
immediately removed from the UK"—in effect providing the
power to detain foreign citizens incommunicado for long periods. When it adopted that provision, the United Kingdom
withdrew from the obligation not to detain individuals without
trial that it had undertaken under the European Convention on
Human Rights. That derogation from European law has been
roundly criticized in Europe and around the world, as critics
point out that of all the countries in Europe—including many
others threatened by terrorism—only the United Kingdom has
felt it necessary to derogate from the treaty principle against
detention without trial. The 2001 act also sought to enhance
the security of aviation and nuclear and scientific sites and laboratories, increased penalties for "crimes aggravated by racial
or religious hatred" and for terrorist hoaxes, and allowed the
freezing of assets that might be used by terrorists at the very
start of investigations.[4]

The British post–September 11 legislation, like the Patriot
Act, is subject to a range of interpretation. For some British
observers, the act "contains a number of reasonable provisions
dealing with important security safeguards."[5] In terms similar
to those used by defenders of the Patriot Act, the British
defenders of the 2001 Anti-Terrorism Act call many of its pro-

visions uncontroversial, a mere updating and gap filling of previous law intended to respond to new technologies and, it is readily admitted, the resurgent threats of terrorism. For the British civil liberties community, the 2001 act only exacerbated the excesses of the 2000 Terrorism Act and increased government power unnecessarily, "the most draconian legislation Parliament has passed in peacetime in over a century."[6] Along with liberal legislators, the liberal press, and others, Britain's largest civil liberties organization, Liberty, has particularly fought against two significant features of the 2001 Anti-Terrorism Act, both at the enactment stage and in their implementation.

The first is the 2001 act's vigorous and inflexible provisions for arbitrary detention, what British civil libertarians called the "power to intern [foreigners in the United Kingdom] on the basis of suspicion, not [of] what a person has done but what an intelligence expert thinks they might do." And the British government put the detention provision to work immediately. The day after the 2001 Anti-Terrorism Act was passed, ten foreign nationals in Britain were taken from their homes to prison, where most remain today, more than two years later. A total of fourteen are now in custody in Belmarsh Prison under the act.

The British press is prohibited from naming most of these detainees, so we only know about a few. One is Mamoud Abu Rideh, whom one lawyer calls "a highly eccentric and damaged individual, albeit one with a burning commitment to helping others, in particular fundraising for charities in Afghanistan." In solitary confinement in Belmarsh Prison, he "deteriorated into a life-threatening state . . . unable to eat and too weak to be out of a wheelchair."[7] Another is Haydar Abu Doha, who is awaiting extradition to the United States on assertions that he collaborated in terrorist attacks on the United States and whose case might be considered even more serious by the

British civil liberties community if either the U.K. or American governments were willing to release any substantial information about him.[8]

Under the 2001 act, none of the Belmarsh detainees is guaranteed the right to a trial. The act does provide for closed hearings on the sufficiency of the evidence against them, and several such hearings have been held. The government calls these closed hearings a necessity to prevent the leakage of information valuable to terrorists. Critics call them shams that are bolstered by mere assertions of links with terrorists rather than the presentation of hard evidence, assertions based partly on information obtained by mistreatment and torture of prisoners in foreign countries. The Belmarsh detentions, in a high security facility and with no hearings scheduled, prompted a visit by investigators from the Council of Europe to England in February 2002. That visit prompted John Wadham, at the time director of Liberty, the most prominent British civil liberties organization, to note "how out of step we are with the rest of Europe in terms of protecting people's rights while still tackling terrorism."[9] Later in 2002, the Council of Europe's Human Rights commissioner denounced both the detentions and the detention power.

There is an appeals process against these detentions, but Britain's civil libertarians charge that there are numerous flaws in that process. The presumption of innocence does not apply to hearings on these detentions. Detainees and their lawyers are not guaranteed access to all the evidence and other materials—including materials from foreign governments—that have formed the suspicion under which they are being detained. Detainees are, in fact, removed from hearings on their own detention when such secret evidence is heard, as are their lawyers.[10] Wadham and other British civil libertarians have complained that these broad provisions are unmatched anywhere else in Europe, including in countries with terrorist threats as direct as in the United Kingdom, and they have continued to call for the Belmarsh detainees to be either released or charged with crimes.

Like their U.S. counterparts, the Liberty group used litigation as well as publicity to make their case against detentions without trial. Liberty represented the detainees before the Special Immigration Appeals Commission in the summer of 2002 and won a ruling that called the detentions unlawful and discriminatory because the new powers applied only to foreign nationals. For a short time it appeared that the detention policy might be weakened or even undone. But in October 2002, the British Home Office won an appeal from the commission's ruling. The Court of Appeal ruled that the detention policy and the section of the 2001 Anti-Terrorism Act authorizing it were not discriminatory, overturning the commission's initial ruling and reinstating the validity of the detentions.[11]

The second major civil libertarian objection to the 2001 act mirrored developments in the United States, though the argument certainly did not originate in the United States. In the words of Liberty, "[O]ther measures have been smuggled into this bill which have nothing to do with terrorism or the events of September 11" but which represented an opportunity for government to incorporate long-sought powers in a situation of perceived emergency. In Wadham's view, these "smuggled" provisions include "allow[ing] the police to take identity photographs by force," "allow[ing] personal and private information to be obtained by the police and others without any controls, checks or safeguards," and "stor[ing] communications data of millions of innocent users, including email and the internet, on the off-chance that it might be of use in the future."[12]

The 2000 and 2001 acts have also led to increasingly

assertive behavior by government officials. The civil liberties lawyer Gareth Pierce described this in chilling terms in a 2003 lecture at the London School of Economics: "[A] knock on the door, an approach in the street, an obstruction in the aisle at Tescos [supermarket], from an individual saying that he was from the Security Services and wanted to obtain . . . information . . . as to whether there was a threat from terrorism and that in exchange considerable help could be given to the obtaining of British citizenship or regularising of immigration status."[13] And a report by several British nongovernmental organizations documented harassment, repeated searches, mass detention of peaceful protestors, prevention of lawful protest, and other measures used against antiwar protestors in 2002 and 2003.[14]

After several years of detention of foreign nationals and debate over the 2001 Anti-Terrorism Act, a parliamentary committee comprised of elected legislators and peers recommended removing the arbitrary detention provisions in a late 2003 report. The committee agreed that some antiterrorist measures would be needed for "some time to come" and warned that finding an appropriate balance between "providing effective powers . . . while protecting individual rights can be difficult." Yet on the question of arbitrary detention the committee was united, recommending that a new way be found to deal with necessary detentions that "does not require the UK to derogate from the right to liberty under the European Convention on Human Rights."[15] In late 2003 the archbishop of Canterbury also issued sharp criticism of the detention policy,[16] and by early 2004 there was renewed discussion of deporting some of the fourteen detainees held at Belmarsh or employing a form of "suspended detention" involving "restrictions and intensive surveillance" rather than additional months or years in Belmarsh Prison. By no means were all the evaluations entirely negative. A parliamentarian named by the home secretary to review the detentions said that he was "'entirely satisfied' the home secretary was right to certify each as suspected international terrorists." But at the same time he also criticized the use of Belmarsh and some of the conditions in which the detainees are held.[17]

Much of this criticism did not seem to faze the Blair government, already under withering attack for allegedly amending and overstating intelligence estimates before the Iraq war. In late 2003, while facing increasing criticism for detentions under the 2001 Anti-Terrorism Act, the Blair government again sought to add to governmental powers, sparking a broader and even more vociferous level of opposition than arose when the 2001 Anti-Terrorism Act was proposed shortly after the September 11 attacks. The government proposed a "civil contingencies" bill that would replace outmoded legislation from the 1940s and 1950s dealing with civil emergencies. The civil contingencies law would confer the power to restrict civil liberties and impose widespread emergency powers, including curfews, prohibiting public meetings and peaceful protest, seizure of property without compensation, forced evacuations, forced quarantines, and forcible control of financial institutions, all on the say-so of the national government.

The bill's broad definition of such an "emergency" originally included events that threaten the "political, administrative or economic stability" of the nation, prompting fear and criticism that a government might employ that definition to protect its own power. British civil libertarians led by Liberty voiced strong criticism: "Everyone accepts that in the event of a major terrorist attack or a natural disaster, the police and armed forces will need to act quickly. . . . But that is no reason for granting the Government a blank check to designate as an emergency anything they deem to be such. . . . [T]his measure could be used to suppress or curb any demonstration or protest. It could . . . be used against countryside alliance supporters marching on London or students protesting top-up [increases in tuition] fees."[18]

A parliamentary committee warned that the broad original wording might allow a government to declare an emergency just "to protect its own existence." After extensive discussions with Liberty and parliamentarians, the government agreed to revise the definition of "emergency" and several other checks so that the government could not use its newly granted powers to respond to political events.[19] Toward the end of this consultative process, the new director of Liberty, Shami Chakrabarti, noted that the "initial proposals were quite terrifying."[20] But she also praised the government, noting that while civil libertarians still objected to some elements of the bill, "there has been a real listening and very detailed engagement." Another civil liberties group, Statewatch, continued to criticize the bill, calling it "truly draconian."[21]

In February 2004, yet another government proposal surfaced that would further strengthen the government's hand in dealing with suspected terrorists. Under this plan, secret trials of suspected terrorists could be held without the presence of a jury, with the burdens of proof reduced from "beyond reasonable doubt" to guilt "on a balance of probabilities." Under this proposal, judges and lawyers would be "vetted" by security agencies, and some evidence would remain unavailable to defendants and their lawyers. A few days later, Prime Minister Blair appeared to give some support to the notion of reducing the standard of proof against alleged terrorists.[22] Understandably, these government discussions drew sharp condemnation from a growing coalition of British civil liberties groups, lawyers, newspapers, and some members of Parliament. Liberty compared these procedures to trials under the communist governments of Eastern Europe and in Saddam Hussein's Iraq.[23]

The United Kingdom has also tried to deal harshly with government employees acting as whistleblowers on classified matters relating to terrorism and war-related intelligence. A translator at the Government Communications Headquarters (GCHQ), one of Britain's intelligence agencies, was charged in 2003 with violations of the British Official Secrets Act for disclosing before the Iraq war that the U.S. National Security Agency had sought the cooperation of British counterparts in eavesdropping on six foreign Security Council delegations before important council deliberations on the Iraq war. The charges against the intelligence analyst, Katherine Gun, were dropped in February 2004.[24] The British government has also sought to close charities linked to terrorist groups, and to extradite one significant individual involved in one of those charities to the United States on terrorism-related charges. Those developments are discussed in chapter 5.

The British debate over antiterrorism policy—and the strength of opposition to Blair government policies—has of course emerged from a different dynamic than in the United States, where close to three thousand people were killed on September 11. British constituencies seeking to slow and constrain British government responses to terrorism have been able to use European Union law as a legal and rhetorical benchmark to constrain the extension of British antiterrorism law and policy. This has become a common tactic in the British debate, one intended partly to broaden an opposition coalition beyond those focused on civil liberties to others concerned with Britain's place in Europe. As John Wadham of Liberty argued in March 2002, for example, against the arbitrary detention provisions in the 2001 Anti-Terrorism Act: "[S]everal European countries have faced direct terrorist threats; several have troops in Afghanistan. Why did only the UK, of the 40-plus countries signed up to the [European] Convention [on Human Rights], deem such extreme measures essential?"[25]

On the other hand, English opponents of severe antiterrorism legislation seem to have been hampered by the difficulties in forming an effective alliance between liberal and conservative activists (of the kind that has been established so effectively on a range of issues in the United States). And, both traditionally and in the current crisis, Britain's committed civil libertarians have perhaps not had the access to resources or legislators that their American colleagues have enjoyed.

Australia

In sharp contrast with the United Kingdom, Australia had "little or no experience of terrorism" before September 2001 and thus had little law on the issue.[26] But the Australian state has been resurgent even without legislation specifically on terrorism, as measured by wiretaps and electronic surveillance of its citizens. Mail investigations took place on more than seventeen thousand Australians in 2002, with requests from nearly sixty government institutions. There were over twenty-five hundred court orders for telephone wiretaps, and government investigation of 733,000 telephone bills.[27]

The immediate Australian state response to the September attacks was to tighten domestic surveillance of suspected terrorists and to introduce a "suite" of antiterrorism legislation in the Australian parliament that enhanced state antiterrorist powers and vested additional discretion and power in the Australian federal attorney general. That suite of legislation included the Security Legislation Amendment (Terrorism) Bill, Suppression of the Financing of Terrorism Bill, Criminal

Code Amendment (Suppression of Terrorist Bombings) Bill, Border Security Legislation Amendment Bill, and Telecommunications Interception Legislation Amendment Bill, all introduced in 2002.[28] The Australian government's view, expressed through an attorney general whose role would be strengthened under the new laws, was that "the community is prepared to take some modest sacrifices of human rights and civil liberties in order to give the government the tools that will . . . assure the public that [it is] protected appropriately.[29] Of all of these proposals, the Security Legislation Amendment (Terrorism) Bill, with provisions to expand government authority, elicited the most opposition within Australia.[30]

Even treason was broadened by the proposed Australian act, consistent with an international trend to expand the definitions of terrorism and terrorist activity to encompass elements of sedition or treason. According to Australian civil liberties groups, the government sought to "politicise" the process of bringing treason charges by requiring direct attorney general intervention, and it sought to criminalize failure "to inform the authorities of a possible act of treason." Such a provision, one civil liberties organization pointed out, could lead to the prosecution of Australians acting to negotiate peaceful resolutions of other nations' civil disputes, as occurred in Sri Lanka.[31] The draft bill also reversed, for terrorism cases, the presumption of innocence.

Despite the attorney general's confidence that these measures would pass, opposition within Australia was immediate and broad. Opponents spanned a broad range of political and legal views, but one unifying position was that new legislation was simply unnecessary and was disproportionate to the terrorist threats to Australia. The president of one of Australia's largest civil liberties groups put it clearly: "The proposed anti-terror laws are founded on a fallacy, a verbal trick. The Government asserts that 'terrorism' is some new species of human malefaction, having its own legal and moral qualities. . . . In fact, 'terrorism' is only another name for serious criminal activity. All that distinguishes a 'terrorist' act from any other criminal act [is] its scale and its political motivation. There is no need for a new offence of terrorism. Our criminal law already provides heavy penalties for the crimes in question—murder and conspiracy to murder in particular."[32]

Opponents forced some changes in the legislation, which finally passed. For example, the very broad definition of "terrorist act" in the government's initial proposal was narrowed to require some element of intentional intimidation or coercion. And the government's reversal of the traditional presumption of innocence in terrorism cases—which would have required detainees to prove that they were not terrorists—was undone under a raft of criticism.[33] Australia's civil libertarians, like those in some other countries, took to attacking draft legislation because it went further than the Patriot Act and Britain's 2001 Anti-Terrorism Act. "The FBI, CIA and MI5 don't have any laws of this sort and haven't asked for any. If this sort of law does not exist in the US and UK, and they don't want it, why are we enacting it, with all the civil liberties downsides?"[34]

In Australia, as in the United States and the United Kingdom, initial government efforts have been followed by a second wave of proposed antiterrorism law and enforcement. In Australia this "second cornerstone of Australia's new anti-terrorism laws," the Australian Security Intelligence Organisation Legislation Amendment (Terrorism) Act 2003 (ASIO Act), was primarily intended to enable the Australian security organizations to detain a range of terrorism suspects or persons who might have some knowledge of potential terrorist activities and to criminalize "withholding of information regarding terrorism."[35] The ASIO Act, tabled in March 2002, elicited vituperative opposition from a range of legislators, civil liberties and human rights organizations, and others throughout Australia,[36] resulting in a delay of more than a year before passage.[37] The final bill was softened to "better protect the human rights of children, including limitations on the periods during which a person can be questioned, and . . . access to a legal representative." And the detention provisions were enacted with a sunset clause. Yet the final bill continued to allow for detention of children between sixteen and eighteen for up to seven days, and Australia's civil libertarians vowed to try to further weaken it.[38]

Until October 2002, Australians were perhaps confident in their sense that they had not yet been directly touched by large-scale terrorism. Australia was affected by the tragedy of September 11, but its own version of September 11 occurred a year later, when a terrorist bombing in Bali, Indonesia, killed eighty-eight Australians.[39] The Bali bombing may have softened the environment for adopting tougher new antiterrorism legislation in Australia, though the passage of time after September 11, as in the United States and the United Kingdom, made it easier to resist such proposals as well.

Australian judges, like their English counterparts on the Court of Appeal and a number of American federal judges in the cases that have come into the U.S. courts since late 2001, have been concerned with aspects of the U.S. response to September 11, particularly the Guantanamo detentions, which included several Australian citizens.[40] As Justice Derrington of the Queensland Supreme Court noted: "Certainly the perpetrators should be pursued and punished with the full force of the law, and all proper preventative measures against further attack should be employed. But the rule of law must not be broken or bent in the process. It must be preserved in its letter and spirit. If law is observed and exalted only when it does not matter, it is a sham. Its need becomes greatest in times when it is under challenge or when there are strong sentiments of revenge and fear. Then, it is wrong to assert that the laws should be suspended or watered down to meet current convenience."[41]

Australian scholars and activists have raised serious questions as to whether Australia's post–September 11 antiterrorism legislation comports with Australia's commitments in international law, just as British and American activists and intellectuals have raised similar questions in their countries. That Australians have been imprisoned at Guantanamo has only fueled these fires. But more important than the challenges under international law have been the dignified and spirited challenges to uphold Australia's traditional vision of the rule of law. Justice Michael Kirby put it well, in a widely read and widely cited speech to the Australian bar, in words that echo usefully in the United States, Britain, and India as well as in Australia.

> The countries that have done best against terrorism are those that have kept their priorities, retained a sense of proportion, questioned and addressed the causes of terrorism, and adhered steadfastly to constitutionalism and the rule of law. . . . Keeping proportion. Adhering to the ways of democracy. Upholding constitutionalism and the rule of law. Defending, even under assault, and even for the feared and hated, the legal rights of suspects. These are the ways to maintain the support and confidence of the people over the long haul. . . . Every erosion of liberty must be thoroughly justified. Sometimes it is wise to pause before acting precipitately. If emergency powers are clearly required, it may be appropriate to subject them to a sunset clause—so that they expire when the clear and present danger passes. . . .
>
> In the course of the century of the Australian Commonwealth, we . . . have made many errors. We have sometimes laughed at and belittled citizens who, appearing for them-

selves, fumbled and could not reach justice. We have sometimes gone along with unjust laws and procedures. We have
occasionally been instruments of discrimination and it is still
there in our law books. We have not done enough for law
reform or legal aid. We have not cared enough for justice.
We have just been too busy to repair the wrongs that we saw.
Yet at critical moments in our nation's story, lawyers have
upheld the best values of our pluralist democracy. In the
future, we must do so more wholeheartedly. To preserve liberty, we must preserve the rule of law. The rule of law is the
alternative model to the rule of terror, the rule of money and
the rule of brute power. That is our justification as a profes-
sion. It is our continuing challenge after 11 September
2001.[42]

By mid-2004 there was increasing Australian concern about
David Hicks, an Australian held at Guantanamo and charged
with conspiracy, attempted murder, and aiding the enemy.
The United States planned to try him before a military tri-
bunal, prompting stronger calls in Australia for Hicks's case to
be adjudicated—as *The Age* (Melbourne) put it—"under Australian law or before a properly constituted international tri-
bunal, not by the U.S. military."[43] An Australian citizen went
on trial in Perth for allegedly conspiring to bomb the Israeli
Embassy in Canberra and reports emerged from that trial
about attacks planned earlier against the Sydney Olympics and
Australia's Jewish community.[44] In addition, new governmental proposals for closed trials of defendants charged with
crimes involving national security prompted concern from
some lawyers groups, including the Law Council of Australia,
as well as the Australian civil liberties community and the
press. The proposed National Security Information (Criminal
Proceedings) Bill would require clearances of lawyers and limit
media coverage and public access to certain trials. The government continued to press for changes to the Commonwealth

Crimes Act that would prevent terrorism suspects from being granted bail and allow police to hold detainees for terrorism-related questioning for twenty-four hours, up from the four hours under current law.[45]

India

In India, political violence has been present since the founding of the republic. Separatist groups continue to dot India; Kashmir remains a major international flash point of continued conflict; terrorism and low intensity war all loom. And India and Pakistan continue to joust across a border that may be second only to the two Koreas for its danger of massive war. Nor is political violence in India limited to separatists, Kashmir, and the Indo-Pakistani conflict: the Indian state itself has committed violence against political opponents, Muslims, and others on a regular basis and has ignored or deemphasized violence committed by its conservative Hindu backers.

It is in that complex environment that the Indian government dominated by the conservative Bharatiya Janata Party responded to the September 11 attacks. The government's immediate response was to criminalize conduct that could be construed as terrorism through a new executive mandate, the Prevention of Terrorism Ordinance, in order to counter what it claimed to be "an upsurge of terrorist activities, intensification of cross border terrorism, and insurgent groups in different parts of the country."[46]

The Prevention of Terrorism Ordinance was drafted quickly and introduced rapidly after the attacks in the United States. It was directly based on earlier, draconian antiterrorist legislation under which thousands had been detained. That earlier legislation, the Terrorist and Disruptive Activities Prevention Act (TADA), had lapsed in the Indian parliament in 1995 when concerned legislators refused to renew it, after a campaign that brought together rights activists, liberal intellectuals, and some parliamentarians. Indian public interest and human rights groups had charged that, under TADA, over sixty-seven thousand persons had been detained and over fifty-nine thousand of those had never had a judicial case brought against them. The greatest number of TADA arrests had been in areas undergoing ethnic, religious, and political conflict—not in the hotbed of Indian terrorist activities, places such as Jammu and Kashmir. One civil liberties group charged that of the more than nineteen thousand detained in Gujarat, for example, a majority were innocent members of non-Hindu religious minority groups.[47]

Following the failures of the TADA law, the government had failed to win adoption of a new Prevention of Terrorism Bill in 2000 under withering criticism from civil liberties groups, the Indian National Human Rights Commission, intellectuals, and opposition political parties. But September 11 provided exactly the spur needed, and the Prevention of Terrorism Ordinance was enacted in late October 2001. In drafting what immediately became known in India as "POTO," the Indian government drew upon new antiterrorism legislation in the United States and Britain to justify the new Indian law, in some cases actually referring to the American and British statutes, as well as to earlier Indian legislation and the failed 2000 terrorism bill.

But the Indian Prevention of Terrorism Ordinance in many ways went further than the initial American and British responses to the crisis. This was quickly noted and emphasized by the government's critics. Without irony—for irony with respect to the Patriot Act and the 2001 U.K. Anti-Terrorism Act can perhaps be only homegrown—this emerging Indian coalition of rights activists, opposition legislators, parts of the media, ethnic and minority activists, and others relied partly on the new American and British legislation to argue for a more relaxed approach in India. Even the Patriot Act, noted Ravi Nair, a prominent Indian human rights activist, did "not alter the [domestic] criminal trial process for terrorism cases, nor does it accord the Executive powers immunised from meaningful judicial review."[48] And while the new Indian legislation allowed for detention of up to half a year, the new British legislation only provided for considerably shorter extensions of arrests of citizens (though, of course, indefinite and incommunicado detention for noncitizen terrorist suspects).

If even the American and British legislation was this limited, the argument went, why was the Indian legislation so stringent? This argument revealed the weaknesses of the Indian opponents of antiterrorism legislation: about the best they could do was to rely upon post–September 11 American and British statutes. Thus it was with no irony that Nair and other opponents of the Indian legislation argued, futilely, that the Prevention of Terrorism Ordinance "must contain a limited and specific definition of terrorism, such as that contained in the Prevention of Terrorism Act of the United Kingdom."[49]

India's opponents of new antiterrorism legislation, much like their colleagues in the United States, Britain, and Australia, were unable to stem the immediate onslaught of post–September 11 legislation. But in India, in contrast at least to the situation in Australia, it was also difficult to slow the juggernaut even briefly or to fight for softening amendments. The Indian Prevention of Terrorism Ordinance was enacted in late 2001, largely in the severe form drafted by the government. It provided broad new definitions of "terrorist acts," mandated the death penalty or life imprisonment for such acts, and permitted sentences of life imprisonment for a range of lesser terrorism-related crimes. Membership in "an organisation . . . concerned with or involved in terrorism" was deemed punishable by life imprisonment, even if the organization was political and nonviolent and even if an individual's membership was unrelated to terrorist operations.

Persons accused under the ordinance could be detained for up to 180 days. The ordinance shifted burdens of proof of innocence to the accused, rather than maintaining the government's traditional burden to prove guilt. The ordinance also allowed the government to maintain the secrecy of witnesses' identities, relaxed rules on admissibility of forced confessions made to police, allowed prosecutors to deny bail, appointed special courts to hear terrorist-related charges, and denied judges most discretion in sentencing. As enacted, the new ordinance was not reviewable for five years, or until 2006.[50]

Public opposition to POTO faded somewhat late in 2001, after a terrorist attack on the Indian Parliament in New Delhi killed nine police and Parliament staff. In the understated words of one Indian civil liberties organization, the December 2001 attack on Parliament "served to blunt . . . opposition to the ordinance."[51]

Although the Prevention of Terrorism Ordinance was valid for five years, it was enacted as a government decree rather than through statutory adoption by Parliament and was thus subject to political attack on that ground. In early 2002, after the terrorist attack on Parliament in Delhi, the government sought to convert the ordinance into a full Prevention of Terrorism Act (POTA) that would incorporate many of the same provisions as the 2001 ordinance but also have the formal endorsement of the national legislature. Despite the attack on Parliament, the first introduction of the Prevention of Terrorism Act failed in the upper house of the Indian parliament because of strong concerns about executive power and distrust of the ruling coalition. Facing increasing opposition, the government was forced to convene a rare joint session of Parliament, only the third since the founding of the republic, as "the only way the government could muster the majority required." After intensive debate and strong opposition from human rights organizations, intellectuals, opposition political parties, and others, the Prevention of Terrorism Act was adopted in March 2002.[52]

The Prevention of Terrorism Act incorporated many of the provisions of the earlier ordinance: an expanded, broad definition of terrorism as well as extension of the act's provisions to murder, robbery, and other crimes if the authorities alleged that the crimes were terrorism related; and criminalization of any association or communication with a suspected or designated terrorist organization or individuals. The act permits the authorities to hold suspects for up to 180 days and to deny bail and then to refuse to provide a jailed defendant with any information as to his or her alleged crime. It allows the government to keep witnesses' identities secret, dangerously increasing the possibility of inappropriate police activity. Much of the act provides criminal sanctions for acts already considered criminal under the Indian Penal Code and other Indian statutes—including murder and other crimes, such as weapons and explosives possession. The act includes mandatory minimum sentencing, severely reducing the role of judges in the sentencing process; allows the police to seize terrorist-related property at their discretion; criminalizes the refusal or unwillingness of government officials or businesspeople to provide information requested by the authorities (with no limits or process on authorities' requests); allows designation of a terrorist organization without providing evidence; and criminalizes the undefined act of providing "support" to a terrorist group.[53]

Confessions made to police under the act are admissible in court, even where they are provided under torture or the threat of mistreatment, without any countervailing pressure upon the police to refrain from torture or other mistreatment. POTA allows wiretapping and other surveillance results to be used against defendants without any approval requirements for the underlying surveillance activities. The act also reconfirms the establishment of special courts to try terrorism-related crimes. These special courts may hold trials in secret and are allowed to diverge from the traditional presumption of innocence in treatment of defendants.

In the words of one Indian civil liberties group: "POTA fails to offer the most basic safeguards for a fair trial and due process of law. The grim tradition of national security legislation in India has revealed that such laws result in maximum human rights violations, for minimum convictions."[54] Those fears were especially heightened in 2002 and 2003, after communal violence devastated the western state of Gujarat. In the wake of the Gujarat violence, which shocked much of India and the world, human rights groups charged that the authorities came down squarely on the side of militant Hindus and that one of the means of isolating and detaining Muslims was the Prevention of Terrorism Act.[55]

All along, the great fear of the Indian liberal opposition was that the new Prevention of Terrorism Ordinance would be "used for preventive detention of . . . peaceful dissenters [rather] than for tackling terrorism."[56] By 2003, even beyond Gujarat, there were strong indications that those fears were being realized. In February 2003, for example, the *Times of India* reported that hundreds of citizens (including some as young as ten years old and as old as eighty-one) had been arrested in the eastern Indian state of Jharkhand on charges of terrorism, in what one nongovernmental organization called "indiscriminate" application of the Prevention of Terrorism Act against indigenous peoples, minority castes, and the political opposition.[57] A total of thirty-two hundred had been named in the state's "first information reports," the precursor to formal criminal charges.[58] In late 2003, the Indian government moved to amend POTA to centralize more power in order to control inconsistent application at state and local levels, but the amendments were greeted with wide mistrust by activists and intellectuals.[59]

By June 2004, the Indian government had reported hundreds of arrests under the Prevention of Terrorism Act, including 234 official arrests in the eastern state of Jharkhand, among them a twelve-year old and an eighty-one-year old who were both released by the new Congress-led government. Significant numbers of arrests were also reported in Jammu and Kashmir, where terrorist attacks have been frequent, and in Gujarat, New Delhi, and other jurisdictions. Human rights groups continued to charge that government arrest reports significantly undercounted the actual use of the act in states throughout India.[60]

The situation became considerably more confused in May 2004, when the Indian Congress Party and its allies scored a stunning upset victory over the BJP in national elections. Congress Party leaders had long expressed doubt over both POTA's severity and its implementation. As Congress leaders Sonia Gandhi and Manmohan Singh formed a new government with Singh as prime minister, the Congress-led coalition announced in early June that the Prevention of Terrorism Act would be "'scrapped' even before it expired" in October, and would not be renewed because "the government was already armed with other Acts to effectively deal with terrorists and infiltrators [and] it had become 'obvious' that certain States . . . were 'misusing'" the act.[61] But in several key states, parties supporting the Prevention of Terrorism Act began enacting new statewide legislation that would mirror the act and allow detentions and other POTA provisions to remain in effect at the state level.[62]

In India, as in the United Kingdom and Australia, the struggle against severe antiterrorism measures in 2003 and 2004 had turned from attempting to ameliorate statutes on initial passage (or even oppose them outright) to tracking their implementation, pointing out violations of basic rights, and seeking to broaden coalitions that might eventually attempt to refuse extensions of the laws or try to constrict their scope. In India, the very informal alliance of human rights and public interest law groups, opposition legislators, nongovernmental organizations, and even the national Human Rights Commission had few firm results to show from its opposition given the power of the Indian state and the ruling coalition, but it could claim to be a visible source of alternative perspectives and constant opposition. In the United Kingdom, civil liberties forces and their allies were arguably stronger, keeping close track of their governments as the governments attempted both to enforce and to expand the antiterrorism laws and policies put into place after September 11.

Conclusion
Antiterrorist Policy & the
New Strategies of Engagement

America's civil libertarians have pursued both traditional and nontraditional strategies to oppose the expansion of some of the more intrusive antiterrorist policies, laws, and programs implemented since September 11. The traditional strategies are well known, and they have been used extensively—litigation, legal defense, public education, and awareness among them.[1] But newer strategies are developing as well, a substantial expansion on those used in the past. A grassroots movement to adopt municipal resolutions of disapproval against the Patriot Act has spread around the country, with over 330 communities in 41 states—representing over 51 million people—passing such resolutions by July 2004.[2] But the most important and most interesting strategy of opposition and resistance has been innovative alliance building. The American Civil Liberties Union (ACLU) and other civil liberties groups have formed coalitions of interest with a range of organizations and constituencies concerned with the implications of post–September 11 policies. Those groups range from conservative and libertarian organizations such as the Cato Institute and

Rutherford Institute, to prominent individuals on the right such as Dick Armey and Bob Barr, to issue-based groups such as gun owners and corporate and business travelers, often aided by conservative columnists and pundits.[3]

At both the state and federal level, the civil liberties community has worked with other constituencies concerned about the uses of governmental power, privacy, and other civil liberties issues long before September 11, including the gun lobby and anti-abortion groups. "Historically, this is not unusual. . . . It has always been clear that those on the conservative side who favor limited government were worried about the loss of privacy," noted one ACLU official.[4]

Those coalitions long predate September 11. At the state level, they included work on privacy, wiretapping, demonstration rights, and other issues with gun owners, anti-abortion and other groups outside traditional liberal constituencies. In North Dakota, for example, a "home-grown movement" led by conservative Republican legislators "seized on a disquiet among the electorate" against widening use of personal information by banks to lead a legislative drive to prohibit disclosure of banking information.[5] At the national level, the civil liberties community worked closely with conservative groups in opposition to the wiretap provisions of the Community Assistance to Law Enforcement Act (CALEA), originally passed in 1994, and other legislation of concern to civil liberties advocates on the liberal and conservative sides of the spectrum.

At the national level, this process of alliance has clearly accelerated since September 11. In the first press conference after the horrific September 11 events, Anthony Romero notes the "concern for civil liberties" was "notable right from the very beginning across the political aisle. . . . Some in the civil liberties wing of the Republican party cared as deeply and as vigorously as anyone on the liberal side." "Once we realized this," says Romero, "we sought to build those relationships."[6] Liberal advocates of civil liberties found common cause with their more conservative colleagues on talk shows, and the opposition of Dick Armey and others to TIA, TIPS, and some elements of the Patriot Act was watched carefully. It was Armey who, in 2002, declared Attorney General Ashcroft and the Justice Department "out of control."[7] And alliances quickly developed with other conservatives deeply concerned about intrusive government and privacy—David Keene and the American Conservative Union, Grover Norquist at Americans for Tax Reform, Phyllis Schlafly at Eagle Forum, and a number of conservative legislators. Romero and Murphy played key roles in this alliance-building effort.

As the civil liberties community began to work to pass local resolutions against the Patriot Act (in addition to the judicial challenges), some of those resolutions came out of conservative areas, such as Alaska and Idaho; the areas were "an interesting mix of Republican and conservative strongholds . . . not just Amherst, Berkeley, and Cambridge," notes the ACLU's Romero. The ACLU and other civil liberties groups have located, occasionally prompted, and prominently featured statements by well-known conservatives and libertarians against aspects of the Patriot Act, CAPPS II, Matrix, TIA, TIPS, and other post–September 11 government efforts. Civil liberties groups have entered into coalitions with right-wing organizations to oppose specific legislation or government programs. The ACLU has even featured military and law enforcement personnel in its marketing campaigns.

Perhaps most well-known have been the ACLU's relationships with former Georgia Congressman Bob Barr and the former House Majority Leader Dick Armey, two icons of the American conservative movement and fierce critics of Bill

Clinton and most liberal causes. Finding common ground in opposing government intrusions on privacy and individual rights, Barr was hired as an ACLU consultant in late 2002, though he had worked with the ACLU's Washington office since 1995. Armey has also worked with the organization. "We have to be realistic about what party's in power," noted Laura Murphy of the ACLU's Washington office when the reports of Armey and Barr's consultancies circulated in late 2002.[8] She amplified her comments for the *Washington Post:* "Bob Barr and the ACLU disagree on many issues, but we have no doubt that a strange-bedfellows collaboration between us will yield great things. . . . If we're going to affect federal policy, we have to have access to Republicans."[9]

There was some weariness to this alliance building within the traditional core civil liberties constituency, though these coalitions have generally been welcomed. When Barr and Armey's work with the ACLU was announced, for example, there were "a number of letters, and some cancelled memberships," according to an ACLU official. Romero calls it "initial skepticism and some hostility." But, he also notes, "people have seen the utility of it." Another ACLU official goes further. "Generally speaking, there is wide acceptance of the notion that we have to reach out to people who may not agree with us all the time, but agree with us on some issues, and who have access to the levers of power on certain issues."

All these currents were in evidence at the ACLU's second national membership conference, held in July 2004 in San Francisco. There was "some hissing" as Bob Barr was introduced to an audience comprised largely of "traditional CLU members and activists." But his rousing, thumping critique of the Patriot Act drew a standing ovation, "a very pronounced difference" from his initial reception. An earlier panel had featured Clinton prosecutor Kenneth Starr and Wayne LaPierre,

executive vice president and chief executive officer of the
National Rifle Association, and they received the same reception—"initial tentativeness, and hostility," notes an ACLU
official who was present. But LaPierre called resoundingly for
an American without "gulags," and other areas of agreement
with traditional civil liberties constituencies became clear during the discussion. "They were greeted at the end," Romero
notes, "with resounding applause." "The mission of protecting
constitutional rights and civil liberties cuts across the political
spectrum," insists Romero. "That doesn't mean you give up
your principles—it means you find common ground. The
AARP defends the rights of the elderly no matter what political stripe they are. . . . The ACLU needs to be seen as defending civil liberties regardless of political ideology."[10]

These are coalitions based on interest, opportunity, and
reaction. They rise and fall with particular issues—resonating
most powerfully on the issues that seem to most closely impli-
cate privacy, such as Total Information Awareness, Operation
TIPS, and the Patriot Act II,[11] and significantly less forcefully
on detainees. Those coalitions have been successful in forcing
retreats on TIA, Operation TIPS, and perhaps Patriot Act II
and in forcing the attorney general and the Justice Department
to take valuable time to engage in a campaign to defend the
Patriot Act and a few second wave programs. Recent efforts to
amend the Patriot Act in Congress also seek to build on these
alliances. One such example of a left-right legislative alliance
on security legislation is the July 2003 vote by the House of
Representatives to strip out "sneak and peek" searches from
the Patriot Act.[12]

It is not yet clear whether this process of coalition building
represents a fundamental reordering of civil liberties work or a
set of responses to particular events—September 11, the
Patriot Act, and some of the second wave policies and pro-

grams. But the work of these individuals and groups has been noticed: the Justice Department and the White House have made significant efforts to oppose and split the emerging alliance of opposition to some of the antiterrorist policies. The Justice Department, for example, seeks to identify opposition specifically with the ACLU and to shore up support for the Patriot Act and second wave policies in conservative and libertarian communities.[13] In turn, of course, those fighting the expansion of security powers also seek to isolate their opponents as ideologues, narrowing the alliance that supports the Patriot Act and second wave initiatives.[14] There have even been initial, quite tentative efforts to bring some affected elements of the business community into the opposition tent on economic grounds. The *New York Times*, for example, has noted booksellers' complaints that section 215 authority to seize business records, including sales of books and other goods, may be having a "chilling effect" on the rapidly growing business of online sales, which is more susceptible to a record trail and government information requests.[15]

In Great Britain, Australia, and India, as chapter 6 shows, resistance to the resurgence of the state and antiterrorism policy has also been increasing. But in those countries alliances with conservative forces have not been as effective as in the United States, either because a libertarian, privacy-oriented community is less prominent or because traditional civil libertarians have not reached out as effectively as their American counterparts. Alliance building on the international front is at the early stages, but it is beginning, including contacts and discussions between the ACLU and the British organization Liberty in the fall of 2003.

There are many aspects to the resurgence of the state through antiterrorism policy and law since the vicious and tragic attacks of September 11. This volume has discussed aspects of that resurgence with particular reference to the second wave of antiterrorism policy; the struggle over policy and law at the state level in the United States; the effects on the academic and nonprofit sectors; and contemporaneous developments in Great Britain, Australia, and India. The development of antiterrorism policy in the United States, as in Britain, Australia, and India, will depend on domestic political factors as well as on perceived vulnerability to future attacks and on whether or not attacks actually occur, and thus the fate of post–September 11 measures and policies is likely to diverge considerably from country to country. But the modes of state intervention—increased authority to monitor individuals and groups; conduct surveillance; demand documents and records; detain individuals; conduct profiling; and make use of data mining and other means of information acquisition—are likely to remain matters of active controversy in the United States and other countries for years and decades to come in the world of the resurgent state after September 11.

Notes

Chapter 1

1. The Further Readings section at the end of this volume lists useful works by these authors and others that focus on the antiterrorist law and policy after September 11.

2. For in-depth legal and scholarly analysis of the Patriot Act and related antiterrorism and civil liberties issues since September 11, see the works listed in the Further Readings at the end of this volume. See also David Cole, "The New McCarthyism: Repeating History in the War on Terrorism," *Harvard Civil Rights–Civil Liberties Law Review* 38 (2003): 1–29; Marcella David, "Avoiding the T-Word: America Can't Treat Abu Ghraib as 'Torture Lite,'" *International Herald Tribune*, May 24, 2004; Diane Marie Amann, "Guantanamo," *Columbia Journal of Transnational Law* 42 (2004): 263–348; "Symposium: Reflections on the Criminal Justice System after September 11," *Ohio State Journal of Criminal Law* 1 (2003): 1–131; Grayson A. Hoffman, "Litigating Terrorism: The New FISA Regime, the Wall, and the Fourth Amendment," *American Criminal Law Review* 40 (2003): 1655–82; Karen Engle, "Constructing Good Aliens and Good Citizens: Legitimizing the War on Terror(ism)," *University of Colorado Law Review* 75 (2004): 59–114; Jordan Paust, "Judicial Power to Determine the Status and Rights of Persons Detained without Trial," *Harvard International Law Journal* 44 (2003): 503–32; Adrien Wing, "Civil Rights in the Post 911 World: Critical Race Praxis, Coalition Building, and the War on Terrorism," *Louisiana Law Review* 63 (2003): 717–57; David Cole, "Judging the Next Emergency: Judicial Review and Individual Rights in Times of Crisis," *Michigan Law Review* 101 (2002–3): 2565–93; Eric Posner and Adrien Vermeule, "Accommodating Emergencies," *Stanford Law Review* 56 (2003): 605–44; Samuel

Issacharoff and Richard H. Pildes, "Between Civil Libertarianism and Executive Unilateralism: An Institutional Process Approach to Rights during Wartime," *Theoretical Inquiries in Law* 5 (2004): 1–45; Mark Tushnet, "Defending Korematsu? Reflections on Civil Liberties in Wartime," *Wisconsin Law Review* 2003 (2003): 273–306.

3. Nancy Chang, *Silencing Political Dissent: How Post–September 11 Anti-Terrorism Measures Threaten Our Civil Liberties* (New York: Seven Stories Press, 2002), 22–23, 37–38.

4. *Ex parte Milligan*, 71 U.S. 2, 120–21 (1866).

5. Chang, *Silencing Political Dissent*, 23.

6. *Schenck v. U.S.*, 249 U.S. 47, 52 (1919).

7. Quoted in Howard Zinn, *A People's History of the United States* (New York: HarperCollins, 1999), 375.

8. Chang, *Silencing Political Dissent*, 39; see also Edwin Palmer Hoyt, *The Palmer Raids, 1919–1920* (New York: Seabury Press, 1969).

9. Quoted in Chang, *Silencing Political Dissent*, 24.

10. Chang, *Silencing Political Dissent*, 25–26.

11. *Korematsu v. United States*, 323 U.S. 214 (1944).

12. See, for example, Tushnet, "Defending Korematsu?"; Chang, *Silencing Political Dissent*, 25–26.

13. *U.S. v. Robel*, quoted in Chang, *Silencing Political Dissent*, 29.

14. For a review of this history, see Chang, *Silencing Political Dissent*, 29–37.

15. Congressional Record (September 13, 2001), available at www.fas.org/sgp/congress/2001/ s091301.html.

16. Ibid.

17. Attorney General Ashcroft, "Attorney General Ashcroft Speaks about the Patriot Act" (prepared remarks, Boise, Idaho, August 25, 2003). Available at www.lifeandliberty.gov.

18. American Civil Liberties Union (ACLU), *What Is the Patriot Act?* www.aclu.org.

19. See, for example, Steven Brill, *After: How America Confronted the September 12 Era* (New York: Simon and Schuster, 2003).

20. "Reading over Your Shoulder: The Push Is on to Shelve Part of the Patriot Act," *Boston Globe*, March 9, 2004; "Patriot Act under Literary Assault," *Pittsburgh Post-Gazette* (PA), April 2, 2004; "Justice Department Blocks Judge's Request; Government Won't Say If It Used Patriot Powers in ACLU Suit," *Detroit News*, May 21, 2004; "Justice Department Should Reveal Use of Patriot Act," editorial, *Detroit News*, May 23, 2004; "You're Being Watched," *Los Angeles Times*, May 26, 2004.

21. Brill, *After*.

22. Human Rights First (Lawyers Committee for Human Rights), *Assessing the New Normal: Liberty and Security for the Post–September 11 United States* (2003), 19.

23. Ibid., 21. Several provisions of the so-called Patriot Act II would further strengthen the power of the federal government to conduct surveillance in the United States through FISA and other mechanisms. When the Patriot Act II came under intense criticism in the spring of 2003, several of the provisions loosening restrictions on wiretapping and surveillance were then added to another congressional proposal, the Victory Act. These developments are discussed in chapter 2.

24. The new guidelines are at www.fas.org/irp/agency/doj/fbi /index.html#2002.

25. *Center for National Security Studies v. U.S. Department of Justice*, 331 F.3d 918 (CA 9, 2003). In January 2004 the Supreme Court declined to review the case.

26. Human Rights First, *Assessing the New Normal*, 38.

27. Ibid., 39.

28. This section relies on reports by Human Rights First, including *Assessing the New Normal*; and also on chapters and articles in the following works: Cynthia Brown, ed., *Lost Liberties: Ashcroft and the Assault on Personal Freedom* (New York: New Press, 2003); Nat Hentoff, *The War on the Bill of Rights and the Gathering Resistance* (New York: Seven Stories Press, 2003); Richard C. Leone and Greg Anrig, Jr., eds., *The War on Our Freedoms: Civil Liberties in an Age of Terrorism* (New York: Century Foundation, 2003); and other volumes and reports cited in the notes and listed in the Further Readings section at the end of this volume.

29. For further information on the Hamdi case, see, e.g., Charles Lugosi, "Rule of Law or Rule by Law: The Detention of Yaser Hamdi," *American Journal of Criminal Law* 30 (2003): 225–78.

30. Human Rights First, *Assessing the New Normal*, 70.

31. For a sad, disturbing, fascinating memoir of Moussaoui's formative years as an émigré in France, see Adb Samad Moussaoui, *Zacarias, My Brother: The Making of a Terrorist* (New York: Seven Stories Press, 2003).

32. The threat of designation as "enemy combatants" has also reportedly been used against other terrorism-related detainees and defendants, including the well-known Lackawanna Six, a group of six Arab Americans who pled guilty to charges that were considerably reduced from the Justice Department's original assertions. According to one of the Lackawanna group's lawyers: "We had to worry about the defendants being whisked out of the courtroom and declared enemy combatants if the case started going well for us. . . . So we just ran up the white flag and folded." Human Rights First, *Assessing the New Normal*, 70.

33. "Justice Department Must Clarify Role in Inquiry," *New York Times*, May 15, 2004.

34. *Hamdi v. Rumsfeld*, No. 03-6696, 124 S.Ct. 2633; *Rasul v. Bush*, Nos. 03-334 and 03-343, 124 S.Ct. 2686; *Rumsfeld v. Padilla*, No. 03-1027, 124 S.Ct. 2711, each decided on June 28, 2004; texts available at www.findlaw.com.

35. Department of Justice, as reported by the Center for Democracy and Technology (www.cdt.org), September 18, 2003; OMB Watch, October 6, 2003.

36. OMB Watch, October 6, 2003.

37. This complex area is well covered by Charles Doyle, *USA Patriot Act Sunset: Provisions That Expire on December 31, 2005*, Congressional Research Service Report RL32186 (January 2, 2004); and Doyle, *USA Patriot Act Sunset: A Sketch*, Congressional Research Service Report RS21704 (January 7, 2004), www.fas.org.

38. Viet Dinh, *Nightline*, ABC News Transcripts, January 9, 2004, www.lexis.com (accessed March 1, 2004).

Chapter 2

1. The draft act and commentaries are at the Center for Public Integrity's web site, www.publicintegrity.org. A commentary is also available at the ACLU web site (www.aclu.org), dated February 14, 2003. See also Center for Public Integrity, *Justice Department Drafts Sweeping Expansion of Anti-Terrorist Act*, February 7, 2003.

2. Draft Domestic Security Enhancement Act, sec. 501.

3. Jack M. Balkin, "A Dreadful Act II," *Los Angeles Times*, February 13, 2003.

4. Quoted in ACLU, *ACLU Opposes Ashcroft Government Surveillance Bill*, March 4, 2003.

5. ACLU, *On Eve of War, New Right-Left Letter Opposes Justice Department Plans for Legislation That Would Diminish Liberty*, March 17, 2003.

6. Ibid.

7. "Patriot 2: The Eyes Have It," *Atlanta Journal-Constitution*, May 11, 2003.

8. *Atlanta Journal-Constitution*, May 11, 2003; "Curtain Goes up on Ashcroft's Patriot Act II," *Houston Chronicle*, June 15, 2003.

9. John Podesta, "Bush's Secret Government," *American Prospect*, September 2003.

10. "Patriot Act, Part II," *New York Times*, September 22, 2003. See also "Despite Assurances, Bush's Antiterror Plan Is Rekindling Concern," *New York Times*, September 14, 2003.

11. "Americans Rise against 'Patriot Act,'" *San Francisco Chronicle*, September 14, 2003; ACLU Interested Persons Memo Updating the Sta-

tus of "Pieces of Patriot II" Proposals, Oct. 8, 2003, www.aclu.org/safe-andfree.

12. See Laura Murphy, "Remarks at the National Press Club" (August 25, 2003); and ACLU, *ACLU Opposes Ashcroft Government Surveillance Bill*, 3. Other useful reports on CAPPS II include ACLU, *The Five Problems with CAPPS II*, August 25, 2003. The quotation describing CAPPS II as the "nation's largest domestic surveillance system" is from "Air Security Focusing on Flier Screening," *Washington Post*, September 4, 2003.

13. "A Suspect Computer Program," *Los Angeles Times*, October 2, 2003.

14. "Standing Watch," *Washington Post*, July 20, 2002.

15. ACLU, *Caught in the Backlash: Stories from Northern California* (2003); *San Francisco Chronicle*, September 28, 2002.

16. Murphy, "Remarks at the National Press Club."

17. "Air Security Focusing on Flier Screening."

18. Ibid.

19. "Intelligence Official Will Lead TSA Profiling Effort," *Washington Post*, December 24, 2002.

20. "Air Security Focusing on Flier Screening."

21. "Intelligence Official Will Lead TSA Profiling Effort."

22. "Air Security Network Advances," *Washington Post*, March 1, 2003; "A Safer Sky or Welcome to Flight 1984?" *New York Times*, March 11, 2003.

23. "Travel Industry and Privacy Groups Object to a U.S. Screening Plan for Airline Passengers," *New York Times*, March 6, 2003.

24. Murphy, "Remarks at the National Press Club."

25. "Passenger Screening Plan Assailed," *Washington Post*, March 26, 2003.

26. For some discussion of the breadth of opposition, see ACLU, *Five Problems with CAPPS II*.

27. "Aviation ID System Stirs Doubts," *Washington Post*, March 14, 2003.

28. "Air Security Network Advances."

29. "Surveillance Proposal Expanded," *Washington Post*, July 31, 2003.

30. ACLU, *Five Problems with CAPPS II*.

31. *New York Times*, November 20, 2003.

32. "U.S. and Europeans Agree on Sharing of Airline Passenger Data," *New York Times*, December 17, 2003. The U.S. statement is at www.dhs.gov; the European statement at europa.eu.int (both accessed February 25, 2004).

33. "TSA May Try to Force Airlines to Share Data," *Washington Post*, September 27, 2003.

34. ACLU, *Legislation Mandating GAO Report on CAPPS II*, February 11, 2004.

35. ACLU, *ACLU Criticizes Plans to Go Forward with CAPPS II*, January 12, 2004; "Screening Terrorists," editorial, *Washington Post*, January 21, 2004. The unfortunate name "Trusted Traveler," an example of the tin ear of government naming of programs after September 11 (see the discussion of Total Information Awareness in chap. 2), was rapidly changed to "Registered Traveler."

36. "Northwest Gave U.S. Data on Passengers," *Washington Post*, January 18, 2004; Electronic Privacy Information Center, January 18, 2004; "Airline Gave Government Information on Passengers," *New York Times*, January 18, 2004.

37. "Top Airline Executives to Discuss Privacy Policy," *Washington Post*, January 21, 2004.

38. "Privacy Issues Slow Updated Airline Security," *New York Times*, April 11, 2004; "U.S., EU Will Share Passenger Records; Ridge Calls Agreement 'Essential,'" *Washington Post*, May 29, 2004; "Flier Registration Program to Be Tested," *Washington Post*, June 17, 2004.

39. As defined in the original TIPS information web page, deleted from the U.S. Citizen Corps web site but retained by the Memory Hole at www.thememoryhole.org (accessed February 15, 2004).

40. "What Is Operation TIPS?" editorial, *Washington Post*, July 14, 2002.

41. "Planned Volunteer-Informant Corps Elicits '1984' Fears," *Washington Times*, July 16, 2002.

42. Jesse Walker, "Roll over, James Madison: Where Have All the Federalists Gone?" *Reason*, November 2002.

43. "Postal Service Snubs Operation TIPS," *CNN*, July 18, 2002, www.cnn.com.

44. "TIPS Jar Half-Empty in Bid for Bay Area Watchdogs," *Argus* (Fremont, CA), September 6, 2002.

45. Department of Justice spokesperson Barbara Comstock, quoted in Robert Levy (Cato Institute), "United We Stand, but We'll Snoop Divided," *Los Angeles Times*, July 22, 2002.

46. Nat Hentoff, "Ashcroft's Master Plan to Spy on Us," *Village Voice*, August 2, 2002.

47. "'There's a Problem When U.S. Deputizes Everyone,'" *Telegraph Herald* (Dubuque, IA), September 18, 2002.

48. Jonah Goldberg, cited in Walker, "Roll over, James Madison."

49. "Private Pilots Enlisted for Security," *Washington Post*, October 10, 2002.

50. "Truck Drivers Are Deputized to Watch Pa. Roads," *Philadelphia Inquirer*, August 9, 2002; "Nation's 3 Million Truckers Enlist in War on Terrorism," *Detroit News*, June 5, 2002.

51. Nat Hentoff, "Ashcroft's Shadowy Disciple," *Village Voice*, November 26, 2002; "Road Signs Spur Calls to Terrorism Tip Line," *Washington Times*, March 26, 2003.

52. "The Hub," *Boston Magazine*, September 2003.

53. See public.afosi.amc.af.mil/eagle/index.asp for general information on the Eagle Eyes program (accessed March 2004; documentation available from the author if these passages are removed from the site).

54. "Air Force Asks Americans to Use Their 'Eagle Eyes,'" *Bossier Press-Tribune* (Bossier, LA), March 13, 2003, www.bossierpress.com.

55. "Eagle Eyes Program Involves Everyone," April 17, 2003, afmc.wpafb.af.mil; see also ascpa.public.wpafb.af.mil (accessed February 20, 2004).

56. "Keep Your Eagle Eyes Open," March 28, 2003, www.dcmilitary.com (accessed February 20, 2004).

57. Brigadier General Eric Patterson, "Eagle Eyes up and Running around Air Force," *Global Reliance Magazine*, May–June 2002, www.dtic.mill/afosi/global/ (accessed February 20, 2004).

58. "DoD Logging Unverified Tips," *Wired*, June 25, 2003. The relationship between Eagle Eyes and Talon is discussed briefly in the *TIG (The Inspector General) Brief*, Department of Defense, September–October 2003, afia.kirtland.af.mil (accessed February 20, 2004).

59. "Air Force Needs Citizens' Help; Onlookers Might Be Able to Spot Suspicious Activity," *Daily News of Los Angeles*, April 14, 2004.

60. Murphy, "Remarks at the National Press Club." Extensive information is available in Defense Department, *Report to Congress Regarding the Terrorism Information Awareness Program*, May 20, 2003; and Department of Defense, Office of the Inspector General, *Information Technology Management: Information Technology Awareness Program (D-2004–033)*, December 12, 2003.

61. John Poindexter, *Overview of the Information Awareness Office*, DARPA, August 2, 2002, www.fas.org.

62. William Safire, "You Are a Suspect," *New York Times*, November 14, 2002.

63. See Department of Defense, *Information Technology Management*, 28–29.

64. Ibid., 2.

65. Ibid., i, ii.

66. But see Anita Ramasastry, "The Safeguards Needed for Government Data Mining," January 7, 2004, www.findlaw.com (and other useful articles by Ramasastry on this web site).

67. "U.S. Pressing for High-Tech Spy Tools," Associated Press, February 22, 2004.

68. "Panel Urges New Protection on Federal 'Data Mining,'" *New York Times*, May 17, 2004; "U.S. Agencies Collect, Examine Personal Data on Americans," *Washington Times*, May 28, 2004.

69. The ACLU web site has a section devoted to the Matrix program, including the useful *Data Mining Moves into the States* (2003), www.aclu.org/matrix. A number of newspaper descriptions have also been published; for one particularly detailed report, see "Matrix Links up Private Data," *Atlanta Journal-Constitution*, October 10, 2003.

70. ACLU, *Data Mining Moves into the States.*

71. "U.S. Backs Florida's New Counterterrorism Database," *Washington Post*, August 6, 2003.

72. ACLU, *Data Mining Moves into the States.*

73. IIR/Seisint, Matrix Facts brochure, www.aclu.org.

74. "Matrix Links up Private Data"; see also "U.S. Backs Florida's New Counterterrorism Database," *Washington Post*, August 6, 2003.

75. "FDLE Will Tap into Multistate Terrorism Data Link," *St. Petersburg Times*, September 16, 2003.

76. Ibid.; "U.S. Backs Florida's New Counterterrorism Database," *Washington Post*, August 6, 2003; "From Drugs to Databases," *Sun-Sentinel* (Ft. Lauderdale, FL), January 11, 2004.

77. "From Drugs to Databases."

78. Ibid.

79. Matrix Michigan Briefing, May 8, 2003, www.aclu.org; "Speedy Database Helps Cops Connect the Dots," *Orlando Sentinel*, August 24, 2003; "Big Brother Virginia," *Washington Post*, August 31, 2003.

80. "U.S. Backs Florida's New Counterterrorism Database."

81. Michigan Matrix Briefing.

82. "U.S. Backs Florida's New Counterterrorism Database."

83. Ibid.; see also Associated Press, September 23, 2003, cited in ACLU, *Data Mining Moves into the States.*

84. Southeastern Legal Foundation, *Stop the Matrix in Georgia*, October 15, 2003.

85. "Fear Real-Life Matrix Will Be Monitoring You," *New York Daily News*, November 23, 2003.

86. "2 More States Back off Matrix," *Atlanta Journal-Constitution*, October 17, 2003.

87. "Matrix Links up Private Data"; "Matrix and Privacy: Debate over Information Hits Close to Home," *Atlanta Journal-Constitution*, October 19, 2003.

88. "Perdue Rethinks Matrix," *Atlanta Journal-Constitution*, October 22, 2003.

89. "Ohio May Join in Multistate Database," *Columbus Dispatch*, Octo-

ber 25, 2003; "Controversial Ohio Law Elicits Questions," *Post* (Athens, OH), University Wire, June 4, 2004.

90. ACLU, *Data Mining Moves into the States*. According to IIR, that number had dropped to six—Connecticut, Florida, Michigan, New York, Ohio, and Pennsylvania—by March 2004, www.iir-global.org (accessed February 20, 2004).

91. ACLU Matrix Issue Brief #2, May 20, 2004, www.aclu.org/privacy; "Anti-Terror Database Got Show at White House," *Washington Post*, May 21, 2004; "Big Brother Database Poses Risk to Privacy," editorial, *Detroit News*, May 26, 2004; "Total Information Awareness II?" *St. Petersburg Times* (FL), May 31, 2004.

Chapter 3

1. Among the best sources of information on post–September 11 state antiterrorism law are the resource materials prepared by the National Conference of State Legislatures (www.ncsl.org), including *Protecting Democracy: America's Legislatures Respond—Overview of State Activity in Response to September 11* (April 2002) and later thematic and state updates. Some information is also available through the Library of Congress (thomas.loc.gov/home/terrorleg.htm) and the Council of State Governments (www.csg.org/csg/default).

2. National Conference of State Legislatures, *Protecting Democracy: America's Legislatures Respond*, v.

3. ACLU, *Insatiable Appetite: The Government's Demand for New and Unnecessary Powers after September 11* (2002), 11.

4. "Frenzy to Adopt Terrorism Laws Starts to Recede," *Wall Street Journal*, March 27, 2002; National Conference of State Legislatures, *State Legislation Addressing Terrorism*, December 2001.

5. This typology is adapted from the very useful National Conference of State Legislatures, *Protecting Democracy: America's Legislatures Respond*.

6. Ibid., 82.

7. "Michigan Lawmakers Seek Balance on Police Power," Gannett News Service, October 11, 2001; "Michigan Moves to Bolster Safety," *Lansing State Journal*, October 18, 2001. I am grateful to William Flory, formerly legislative counsel with the ACLU of Michigan, for discussions of the situation in Michigan.

8. Interview with William Flory, February 24, 2004.

9. *ACLU of Michigan Civil Liberties Newsletter*, October 2001.

10. "Legislators Push for Laws to Spy," *Detroit News*, November 1, 2001.

11. See, for example, "State's Terror Legislation Is Premature," edito-

rial, *Port Huron Times Herald* (Port Huron, MI), December 11, 2001; "State Proposes List of New Anti-Terrorism Protections," *Lansing State Journal*, December 12, 2001; ACLU of Michigan, *ACLU Warns Legislature to Proceed Cautiously*, January 24, 2002.

12. "State Lawmakers Pass Wiretap Measure," *Lansing State Journal*, January 30, 2002.

13. See, for example, "Any State Wiretap Law Would Be Tailor-Made," *Detroit News*, March 1, 2002.

14. Telephone interview with William Flory, February 24, 2004.

15. "House, Senate Wrap up Session," *Detroit News*, November 28, 2001.

16. Telephone interview with William Flory, February 24, 2004.

17. ACLU of Michigan, *ACLU Warns Legislature to Proceed Cautiously*.

18. ACLU of Michigan, *Anti-Terrorism Legislation*, January 28, 2002.

19. *ACLU of Michigan Civil Liberties Newsletter*, February 2002.

20. Telephone interview with William Flory, February 24, 2004.

21. *ACLU of Michigan Civil Liberties Newsletter*, July 2002.

22. "Drug Raid Causes Concerns," *Detroit News*, August 1, 2002.

23. For an excellent short review of the Michigan package of antiterrorism initiatives, see Karen Dunne Woodsie and Alan Gershel, "The U.S.A. Patriot Act and Michigan's Anti-Terrorism Laws," *Michigan Bar Journal* 82 (February 2003): 20–23.

24. *ACLU of Michigan Civil Liberties Newsletter*, July 2002.

25. *ACLU of Michigan Civil Liberties Newsletter*, March 2003.

26. Ibid.

27. The ACLU's Freedom of Information request to Michigan authorities and the documents received are at www.aclu.org/matrix. Additional documents are at www.aclumich.org.

28. The text of the November 5, 2003, Matrix meeting is at www.aclu.org/matrix.

29. "The potential for abuse outweighs any benefit in fighting terror, and Michigan should withdraw from the program," wrote the *Detroit News*. See "Big Brother Database Poses Risk to Privacy," editorial, *Detroit News*, May 26, 2004. On recent Matrix developments, see "Is Michigan Spying on You?" *ACLU of Michigan News*, December 2003; Cynthia L. Webb, "Homeland Security Growing Pains," Washingtonpost.com, April 1, 2004; "Database Measured 'Terrorism Quotient,'" eWeek.com, May 21, 2004; "Privacy and the Matrix (Discussion with Barry Steinhardt, ACLU)," Washingtonpost.com, May 27, 2004. For a defense of Matrix, see Heather MacDonald, "What We Don't Know Can Hurt Us," *City Journal* (The Manhattan Institute) (spring 2004): 14–31.

30. "State Legislature Approves Tough Anti-Terrorism Laws," *New*

York Law Journal, September 18, 2001. For a later recap, see "Frenzy to Adopt Terrorism Laws Starts to Recede."

31. The ambiguities and complexities of the Lackawanna case are described vividly in Matthew Purdy and Lowell Bergman, "Unclear Danger: Inside the Lackawanna Terror Case," *New York Times,* October 12, 2003.

32. National Conference of State Legislatures, *State Legislation Addressing Terrorism* (December 2001).

33. "State Legislature Approves Tough Anti-Terrorism Laws." The 2001 New York statute is discussed in Richard Greenberg and Steven Yurowitz, "Analyzing New York's Anti-Terrorism Statute," *New York Law Journal,* May 13, 2002.

34. "Pataki Proposes Terrorism Bill," *New York Law Journal,* November 2, 2001.

35. Jerrold L. Steigman, "Reversing Reform: The Handschu Settlement in Post–September 11 New York City," *Journal of Law and Policy* 11 (2003): 745–99.

36. Testimony of Robert Perry on Behalf of the New York Civil Liberties Union before the New York State Assembly Standing Committee on Health and the Standing Committee on Codes Concerning the Model State Emergency Health Powers Act, March 14, 2002, www.nyclu.org.

37. Ibid.

38. See *The Model State Emergency Health Powers Act, State Legislative Activity,* prepared by the Center for Law and the Public's Health (www.publichealthlaw.net/Resources/Modellaws.htm). For a defense, see Lawrence O. Gostin, Jason W. Sapsin, Stephen P. Teret, Scott Burris, Julie Samia Mair, James G. Hodge, Jr., and Jon S. Vernick, "The Model State Emergency Health Powers Act: Planning for and Response to Bioterrorism and Naturally Occurring Infectious Diseases," *Journal of the American Medical Association* 288 (2002): 622–28. For a critique, see H. Jack Geiger, "Protecting Civil Liberties" and "Public Health and Civil Liberties: A Critique of the Model State Emergency Health Powers Act," in *Terrorism and Public Health: A Balanced Approach to Strengthening Systems and Protecting People,* ed. Barry Levy and Victor Sidel (New York: Oxford, 2003).

39. "Pataki's Bill on Terrorism Passes Senate," *New York Times,* February 12, 2003. A strongly worded critique is "How Albany Drafts a Media Event," editorial, *New York Times,* February 13, 2003. Detailed information on the 2003 New York bill is available in *Legislative Memo: Anti-terrorism Package,* www.nyclu.org; and Bob Perry, "September 11 Opportunism," *NY Civil Liberties,* summer 2003, www.nyclu.org.

40. See, for example, New York Civil Liberties Union, *Rights Advocates*

Raise Strong Objections to New Antiterrorism Legislation, www.nyclu
.org/antiterror_03/203.html, March 12, 2003.

41. "State Bar Attacks Parts of Terrorism Legislation," *New York Law Journal*, April 3, 2003.

42. "A Summary of the Major Actions of the Legislature's 226th Session," *New York Times*, June 29, 2003.

43. "Pataki Calls for Stronger Laws to Fight Crime and Terrorism," *New York Times*, January 8, 2004; "State of the Governor," *New York Times*, January 8, 2004.

44. "Bush Visit Buoys Pataki on Antiterror Legislation," *New York Times*, May 1, 2004. See testimony of Udi Ofer, New York Civil Liberties Union, before New York City Council Committee on Immigration regarding "Overseeing Impact of Antiterrorism Initiatives on Immigrant Communities" (February 11, 2004), at www.nyclu.org. For other recent developments in the New York situation, see "Raw Politics and Rawer Nerves Accompany Albany Terror Debate," *New York Times*, March 17, 2004; "Silver Offers Antiterror Plan as Feud with Pataki Grows," *New York Times*, March 24, 2004. New York's Governor Pataki was able to move ahead with a statewide emergency response communications network through a contract awarded in April 2004, though New York's environmentalist community threatened lawsuits over plans to build tall transmission towers in the Adirondacks. On the statewide communications system, see "Emergency Radio to Span New York," *New York Times*, May 1, 2004.

45. Kimberly A. Felix, "Weapons of Mass Destruction: The Changing Threat and the Evolving Solution," *McGeorge Law Review* 34 (winter 2003): 391–97.

46. Ibid.; National Conference of State Legislatures, *Protecting Democracy* (December 2001).

47. Felix, "Weapons of Mass Destruction."

48. ACLU of Northern California, *ACLU Responds to Governor Davis's State of the State Message*, January 10, 2002.

49. *Newsbytes*, January 16, 2002; *ACLU of Northern California News*, March/April, 2002.

50. "Governor Signs Crucial Reproductive Rights Bill—Vetoes Other Key Measures," *ACLU of Northern California News*, November/December 2002.

51. Sacramento Report, *ACLU of Northern California News*, May 2002.

52. "ACLU Sues Major Airline over Discrimination" and "ACLU to Lockyer: Protect Our Privacy!" *ACLU of Northern California News*, summer 2002.

53. "Spying: State Rules Tougher; State, Feds Differ on Spying," *Long Beach Press Telegram*, October 17, 2003.

54. "Lockyer: Don't Link Activists, Terrorists," *Oakland Tribune*, May 21, 2003; "Lockyer Shakes up Anti-terror Agency," *Oakland Tribune*, May 23, 2003; "How Far Is Too Far to Halt Terror?" *Oakland Tribune*, June 1, 2003; "State's Terror Analysts Reined In," *Oakland Tribune*, June 15, 2003; "Lockyer's Spying Reforms Not Enough, Activists Say," *Oakland Tribune*, August 3, 2003.

55. "California 'Anti-Terror' Databases Unchecked," Znet, www.zmag.org, July 3, 2003.

56. For reforms ordered to CATIC, and activists' responses, see the articles noted in note 54.

57. "California 'Anti-Terror' Databases Unchecked."

58. Ibid.

59. "Frenzy to Adopt Terrorism Laws Starts to Recede"; Rekha Basu, "Americans Forget Some Lessons in Freedoms, Rights," *Des Moines Register*, September 1, 2002.

60. "Frenzy to Adopt Terrorism Laws Starts to Recede."

61. "ICLU Fears Excess in Wake of 9–11," *Des Moines Register*, October 28, 2001.

62. "Frenzy to Adopt Terrorism Laws Starts to Recede."

63. Ibid.

64. In some states, such as Arizona, legislation has been proposed to "conform" state law to the Patriot Act, extending many of the federal government's prerogatives under the Patriot Act to the state governments as well. Those initiatives often also have failed.

Chapter 4

1. Testimony of Sara Melendez, Independent Sector, to the House Committee on Ways and Means, Subcommittee on Oversight, November 8, 2001, www.independentsector.org. For a useful look at post–September 11 giving and charitable activity, see *September 11: Perspectives from the Field of Philanthropy* (New York: Foundation Center, 2001). Other resources are provided at Foundation Center, *Philanthropy's Response to September 11: A Resource List*, www.fdncenter.org. A later report criticized the "leadership vacuum" among nonprofits active in the post–September 11 relief and reconstruction efforts, while praising some organizations' activities. See Michael F. Melcher with Alec Mandl, "The Philanthropic Response to 9/11: A Practical Analysis with Recommendations" (2003); Debra Blum, "Review of 9/11 Response Finds Charities Missed Opportunity to Lead," *Chronicle of Philanthropy*, December 11, 2003.

2. On this problem of "angry donors," see Stephen G. Greene, "Seeking Control in Court," *Chronicle of Philanthropy*, November 28, 2002.

3. On the American Red Cross story, see (among many articles) Grant Williams, "Turmoil at the Red Cross," *Chronicle of Philanthropy*, November 1, 2001; and Deborah Sontag, "Who Brought Bernadine Healy Down?" *New York Times Magazine*, December 23, 2001.

4. On these issues and for references to a range of other views, see Mark Sidel, "The Nonprofit Sector and the New State Activism," *Michigan Law Review* 100 (May 2002): 1312–35.

5. "F.B.I. Raids 2 of the Biggest Muslim Charities," *New York Times*, December 15, 2001.

6. See, for example, "Some Charities Suspected of Terrorist Role," *New York Times*, February 19, 2000.

7. See, for example, "Muslims Ask Where They Can Send Donations," *Chicago Sun-Times*, April 21, 2003; "Muslims Hesitating on Gifts as U.S. Scrutinizes Charities," *New York Times*, April 17, 2003; "In U.S., Muslims Alter Their Giving," *Washington Post*, January 4, 2003; "Florida Arrest Renews Debate over Muslim Charities," *Washington Post*, December 7, 2002; "Muslim Charities Accuse Government of Harming Their Fund Raising," *Chronicle of Philanthropy*, January 9, 2003.

8. The Muslim Public Affairs Council and other organizations have worked extensively on this issue.

9. "After Indictment, Protesters Rally," *New York Times*, October 10, 2002.

10. "Islamic Charity Still Faces Charges," *New York Times*, May 14, 2002.

11. "Charity Tied to Terror," *New York Times*, May 1, 2002.

12. "Bin Laden Relative Linked to '93 Trade Center Bombers," *New York Times*, May 2, 2002; "After Sept. 11, a Little-Known Court Has a Greater Role," *New York Times*, May 3, 2002.

13. "Islamic Charity Still Faces Charges"; "U.S.-Based Charity Is under Scrutiny," *New York Times*, June 14, 2002.

14. "Federal Judge Drops Charges of Perjury in Chicago," *New York Times*, September 14, 2002.

15. "U.S. Indicts Head of Islamic Charity in Qaeda Financing," *New York Times*, October 10, 2002. See also "After Indictment, Protestors Rally."

16. Salam Al-Marayati, "Indict Individuals, Not Charities," *New York Times*, October 11, 2002.

17. "Charity Leader Accepts a Deal in a Terror Case," *New York Times*, February 11, 2003.

18. "3 Muslim Charities No Longer Tax-Exempt," *New York Times,* November 15, 2003.

19. Among many articles, see, for example, "Some Charities Suspected of Terrorist Role," *New York Times,* February 19, 2000.

20. "F.B.I. Raids 2 of the Biggest Muslim Charities"; "U.S.-Based Muslim Charity Raided by NATO in Kosovo," *New York Times,* December 18, 2001.

21. "Transcripts Offer First Look at Secret Federal Hearings," *New York Times,* April 22, 2002.

22. Ibid.

23. "Judge Rules the Hearing for a Detainee Must Be Open," *New York Times,* April 4, 2002; "Danny Hakim, Court Weighs Opening of an Immigration Hearing," *New York Times,* April 11, 2002.

24. "Transcripts Offer First Look at Secret Federal Hearings."

25. "A Court Backs Open Hearings on Deportation," *New York Times,* August 27, 2002; "Excerpts from the Ruling against Secret Hearings," *New York Times,* August 27, 2002.

26. "A Court Backs Open Hearings on Deportation"; "A Win for Open Trials," editorial, *New York Times,* August 28, 2002.

27. "U.S. Defends Secret Evidence in Charity Case," *New York Times,* October 30, 2002.

28. "Asylum Denied to Co-Founder of Foundation," *New York Times,* November 24, 2002.

29. "U.S. Deports Charity Leader in Visa Dispute," *New York Times,* July 16, 2003.

30. "Deportation for Terror Suspect's Family," *New York Times,* July 29, 2003.

31. "3 Muslim Charities No Longer Tax-Exempt."

32. "Prosecutors Link Smuggler to Terrorism," *New York Times,* November 28, 2003.

33. "After a Long, Slow Climb to Respectability, a Muslim Charity Experiences a Rapid Fall," *New York Times,* December 10, 2001.

34. "Some Charities Suspected of Terrorist Role," *New York Times,* February 19, 2000.

35. "Muslim Group Can Be Sued, Judges Decide," *New York Times,* June 6, 2002.

36. "8 Groups in U.S. Protest Bush Move against Foundation," *New York Times,* December 5, 2001; "Bush Freezes Assets of Biggest U.S. Muslim Charity, Calling It a Deadly Terror Group," *New York Times,* December 5, 2001.

37. Ibid. See also "In Texas, Donors to Muslim Charity Seethe at Raids by Government," *New York Times,* December 6, 2001.

38. "8 Groups in U.S. Protest Bush Move against Foundation"; "In Texas, Donors to Muslim Charity Seethe at Raids by Government."

39. "Large Charity Blocks Funds to Several Islamic Groups," *New York Times*, December 7, 2001.

40. "After a Long, Slow Climb to Respectability, a Muslim Charity Experiences a Rapid Fall."

41. "Group Sues Over Frozen Assets, Saying U.S. Violated Rights," *New York Times*, March 9, 2002.

42. "Court Upholds Freeze on Assets of Muslim Group Based in U.S.," *New York Times*, June 21, 2003.

43. "3 Muslim Charities No Longer Tax-Exempt."

44. See, for example, "U.S. Islamic Charities Fear Slump as Ramadan Begins," *San Francisco Chronicle*, November 5, 2002; "Muslims Fear Freeze's Effect," *Tampa Tribune* (Tampa, FL), December 5, 2001.

45. Richard Moyers, "A Shocking Silence on Muslim Charities," *Chronicle of Philanthropy*, October 17, 2002. For a related view, see Al-Marayati, "Indict Individuals, Not Charities."

46. Moyers, "A Shocking Silence on Muslim Charities."

47. Ibid.

48. "Raids Seek Evidence of Money-Laundering," *New York Times*, March 21, 2002.

49. "Muslims Hesitating on Gifts as U.S. Scrutinizes Charities," *New York Times*, April 17, 2003.

50. "Muslim Charity Is Tied to Terror Group," *New York Times*, May 30, 2003.

51. Al-Marayati, "Indict Individuals, Not Charities." See also articles cited in note 7.

52. Ibid.

53. See OMB Watch, *The USA Patriot Act and Its Impact on Nonprofit Organizations* (September 2003), www.ombwatch.org; *Independent Sector Analysis of the Patriot Act's Effects on the Nonprofit Sector*, www.independentsector.org.

54. "IRS Keeps Watch on Relief Charities," *Chronicle of Philanthropy*, March 21, 2002.

55. Executive Order 13224, issued by President Bush on September 20, 2001, www.usig.org (accessed March 4, 2004).

56. "Part of Patriot Act Is Struck Down," *Washington Post*, January 27, 2004; "Judge Rules against Patriot Act," *Los Angeles Times*, January 27, 2004. The Justice Department statement was issued on January 26, 2004, www.usdoj.gov.

57. See testimony of Daniel Bryant, Assistant Attorney General, and Robert W. Chesney, Wake Forest University School of Law, before the

Senate Judiciary Committee hearing on "Aiding Terrorists—An Examination of the Material Support Statute," May 5, 2004, available at judiciary.senate.gov.

58. *Anti-Terrorist Financing Guidelines: Voluntary Best Practices for U.S.-Based Charities*, U.S. Department of the Treasury, Office of Foreign Assets Control, October 17, 2001. The guidelines and the press release are available at www.treas.gov/press/releases/po3607.htm and www.usig .org (accessed March 4, 2004).

59. Al-Marayati, "Indict Individuals, Not Charities."

60. Key documents discussing these developments are Betsy Buchalter Adler and Thomas Silk, *U.S. Treasury's Proposed Voluntary Guidelines for U.S.-Based Charities* (Silk, Adler and Colvin law firm, November 2002); Timothy R. Lyman, Michael G. Considine, and Jennifer L. Sachs, "International Grantmaking after September 11: Dealing with Executive Order 132245 and the USA Patriot Act," Council on Foundations, *International Dateline*, fall 2002; Barnett Baron, "Executive Order, Patriot Act, and Voluntary Guidelines" (e-mail message from the executive vice president of the Asia Foundation to philanthropic leaders and researchers), January 2, 2003; William P. Fuller and Barnett Baron, "How War on Terror Hits Charity," *Christian Science Monitor*, July 29, 2003; Barnett Baron, *Deterring Donors: Anti-Terrorist Financing Rules and American Philanthropy* (Asia Foundation, October 2003); Helmut Anheier and Siobhan Daly, *The Future of Global Philanthropy and Anti-Terrorism Measures: Perspectives from Europe* (UCLA, 2003); Barnett Baron, "Deterring Donors: Anti-Terrorist Financing Rules and American Philanthropy," *International Journal of Not-for-Profit Law*, January 2004 (www.icnl.org). Excerpts from comments on the "voluntary guidelines" provided to the IRS are at the *Chronicle of Philanthropy*, August 7, 2003.

61. Baron, "Executive Order, Patriot Act, and Voluntary Guidelines."

62. See also Nina J. Crimm, "High Alert: The Government's War on the Financing of Terrorism and Its Implications for Donors, Domestic Charitable Organizations, and Global Philanthropy," *William and Mary Law Review* 45 (2004): 1341–1451; Sahar Aziz, "The Laws on Providing Material Support to Terrorist Organizations: The Erosion of Constitutional Rights or a Legitimate Tool for Preventing Terrorism?" *Texas Journal on Civil Liberties and Civil Rights* 9 (2003): 45–91.

63. Debra Morris, "Charities and Terrorism: The Charity Commission Response," *International Journal of Not-For-Profit Law* (September 2002), www.icnl.org.

64. John Stoker, "Weeding out the Infiltrators," *Guardian* (U.K.), February 28, 2002.

65. Ibid.

66. Charity Commission, *Charity Commission Policy on Charities and Their Alleged Links to Terrorism* (May 2002), www.charity-commission.gov.uk/tcc/terrorism.asp.

67. Charity Commission, *Operational Guidance: Charities and Terrorism*, *OG 96-28* (January 2003).

68. Charity Commission, *Charities Working Internationally* (2003).

69. Charity Commission, *Inquiry Report, North London Central Mosque Trust* (2003); "British Arrest Radical Cleric U.S. Seeks," *New York Times*, May 28, 2004. See also extensive coverage of the Abu Hamza case in British newspapers, especially the *Times* (London) and the *Guardian*, in May and June 2004.

70. Charity Commission, *Inquiry Report, Society for the Revival of Islamic Heritage* (2002).

71. Charity Commission, *Inquiry Report, Minhaj-Ul-Quran UK* (2003).

72. "More Than 300 Nonprofit Groups Protest a Federal Proposal on Advocacy," *Chronicle of Philanthropy*, February 19, 2004.

73. The foundation's press release and its president's letter to Representative Nadler are at www.fordfound.org/news/view_news_detail .cfm?news_index=85. Nadler's reaction is at www.house.gov/apps /list/press/ny08_nadler/2003_11_18_ford.html. Useful commentary is "Ford Foundation Cuts Aid to Controversial Charity," *Chronicle of Philanthropy*, November 27, 2003; see also a series of critical articles in the *New York Sun*.

74. The text from the Ford and Rockefeller letters appears in "U. of C., 8 Other Top Schools Say Grant Rules Stifle Academic Freedom," *Chicago Sun-Times*, May 7, 2004; "Stanford Protests Grants' Anti-Terrorism Restrictions," *Stanford Daily*, May 19, 2004.

Chapter 5

1. Useful materials on the effects of antiterrorism in the academic arena include a report by the American Association of University Professors (AAUP), *Academic Freedom and National Security in a Time of Crisis* (October 2003), www.aaup.org; Genevieve J. Knezo, *Possible Impacts of Major Counter Terrorism Security Actions on Research, Development, and Higher Education*, Congressional Research Service Report RL31354 (April 2002). The *Chronicle of Higher Education*, Association of American Universities (www.aau.edu), American Association for the Advancement of Science (www.aaas.org), Federation of American Scientists (www.fas.org), and *Science* magazine regularly publish helpful information on these issues.

2. See, for example, "U.S. Tightening Rules on Keeping Scientific Secrets," *New York Times*, February 17, 2002; MIT, *In the Public Interest:*

Report of the Ad Hoc Faculty Committee on Access to and Disclosure of Scientific Information (June 2002); Dana Shea, *Balancing Scientific Publication and National Security Concerns: Issues for Congress,* Congressional Research Service Report RL31695 (January 2003).

3. AAUP, *Academic Freedom and National Security in a Time of Crisis.*

4. The text of the subpoena itself is posted at webapp.utexas.edu /blogs/bleiter/. Useful newspaper reports may be found in the *Des Moines Register* each day from February 5 to 12 and in Associated Press coverage of the incident, which appeared in many newspapers across the nation. See also the exceptionally useful article by Sharon Walsh, "The Drake Affair," *Chronicle of Higher Education,* March 5, 2004; as well as "University Records on Antiwar Meeting Sought," *Washington Post,* February 8, 2004; "Federal Judge Orders Drake U. to Turn over Information on Antiwar Meeting," *Chronicle of Higher Education,* February 9, 2004; "McCarthyism Watch: Crackdown in Des Moines," *Progressive,* February 9, 2004. The National Lawyers Guild's response to the grand jury subpoena is at www.nlg.org.

5. The text of the gag order, provided by staff at the Drake University Law School, is on file with the author.

6. The Texas incident was first reported by the ACLU. See ACLU, *Feds Respond to Backlash, Quash Iowa Protestor Subpoenas,* February 10, 2004, www.aclu.org; "UT Islam Conference Prompts Army Investigation," Associated Press (published in *Fort Worth Star-Telegram* and elsewhere), February 14, 2004; "Presence of Army Agents Stirs Furor," *Houston Chronicle,* February 14, 2004; "Students Protest Probe of Islamic Conference," Associated Press, February 16, 2004; "Texas Campus Is Puzzled by Federal Agents' Inquiry into Conference on Islam," *Chronicle of Higher Education,* March 5, 2004; personal communications with conference organizer.

7. See "An Antiwar Forum in Iowa Brings Federal Subpoenas," *New York Times,* February 10, 2004; "Anti-War Inquiry Unrelated to Terror," *Des Moines Register,* February 10, 2004; "Prosecutors: Subpoenas Linked to Trespassing Case, Not Anti-War Rally," Associated Press, February 10, 2004.

8. *Harkin Calls on Ashcroft to Address Civil Liberties Concerns in Drake Case,* Harkin press release, February 10, 2004, harkin.senate.gov; Senator Grassley's concerns are noted in the *Des Moines Register* reports.

9. "Federal Prosecutors Back off in Peace Probe," *Des Moines Register,* February 10, 2004 (which includes the Drake president's comments); ACLU, *Feds Respond to Backlash, Quash Iowa Protestor Subpoenas;* "Subpoenas on Antiwar Protest Are Dropped," *New York Times,* February 11, 2004; "U.S. Officials Drop Activist Subpoenas," *Des Moines Register,* Feb-

ruary 11, 2004; "Drake Subpoena Concerns President," *Des Moines Register*, February 11, 2004. The Drake president's views are clearly stated in a statement issued February 10, 2004, at www.drake.edu/newsevents.

10. Personal communication.

11. "Army Intelligence Agents Inquire about UT Islam Conference," *News 8 Austin*, February 12, 2004, www.news8austin.com.

12. "Presence of Army Agents Stirs Furor."

13. "Students Protest Probe of Islamic Conference"; "A Rare but Needed Apology," *San Antonio Express-News*, March 17, 2004.

14. "Academia Becomes Target for New Security Laws," *Christian Science Monitor*, September 24, 2002.

15. Knezo, *Possible Impacts of Major Counter Terrorism Security Actions.*

16. "Academia Becomes Target for New Security Laws."

17. House Committee on Science, *Conducting Research during the War on Terrorism: Balancing Openness and Security, Hearing before the Committee on Science*, 107th Cong., 2d sess., October 10, 2002, segment 2, 12, commdocs.house.gov/committees/science.

18. Knezo, *Possible Impacts of Major Counter Terrorism Security Actions.*

19. See "Letter from the American Council on Education (on behalf of other organizations) to the Department of Homeland Security: Comments on the Proposed SEVIS Fee Collection Process," December 10, 2003, www.acenet.org (accessed March 1, 2004).

20. See Rosemary Jenks and Steven A. Camarota, *Falling behind on Security: Implementation of the Enhanced Border Security and Visa Entry Reform Act of 2002* (December 2003), www.cis.org. An excellent source for information on the SEVIS program is the web page maintained by the NAFSA: Association of International Educators, www.nafsa.org.

21. University of Iowa news release, February 26, 2004. For additional analysis, see Victor C. Romero, "Noncitizen Students and Immigration Policy Post-9/11," *Georgetown Immigration Law Journal* 17 (2003): 357–67.

22. House Committee, *Conducting Research during the War on Terrorism*, segment 2, 10.

23. Ibid., segment 2, 1.

24. Ibid., segment 2, 2. There may also be continuing concern on the part of U.S. consular officers abroad that they may be held criminally responsible for the inadvertent issuance of a visa to a person who engages in a terrorist act in the United States. "Visa Statement," *Scientist*, December 17, 2002.

25. For a useful review of the registration program, see Human Rights First, *Assessing the New Normal* (see chap. 1, n. 22).

26. House Committee, *Conducting Research during the War on Terrorism*, segment 1, 10.

27. "Academia Becomes Target for New Security Laws"; House Committee, *Conducting Research during the War on Terrorism*, segment 1, 7, n. 17. A clear statement of the administration's position on a range of the visa, student, and scholar issues is the speech by John Marburger, director of the Office of Science and Technology Policy in the White House, at the American Association for the Advancement of Science, Science and Technology Policy Colloquium, April 10, 2003, www.ostp.gov.

28. "Visa Statement."

29. Remarks by White House science adviser John Marburger to the National Academies of Science Roundtable on Scientific Communication and National Security, June 19, 2003, www.ostp.gov.

30. See *National Academies' Report on Post–September 11 Scientific Openness at Universities* and transmittal letter, February 6, 2002, www.aau.edu.

31. Ibid.

32. MIT, *In the Public Interest*; House Committee, *Conducting Research during the War on Terrorism*, segment 2, 62

33. Knezo, *Possible Impacts of Major Counter Terrorism Security Actions.*

34. The November 1, 2001, Rice letter to Brown is at www.fas.org, as is the text of NSDD-189.

35. On these issues, see *Sensitive Security Information and Transportation Security*, Congressional Research Service Report RS21727 (February 2004); *"Sensitive but Unclassified" and Other Federal Security Controls on Scientific and Technical Information*, Congressional Research Service Report RL31845 (June 2003); AAUP, *Academic Freedom and National Security in a Time of Crisis*, n. 1.

36. The Card memorandum and other executive branch documents are cataloged at www.fas.org/sgp/bush.

37. AAUP, *Issue Brief: "Sensitive but Unclassified Information"* (December 2003).

38. Federation of American Scientists, FAS Project on Government Secrecy, *Secrecy News*, September 3, 2002.

39. National Academies, *Statement on Science and Security in an Age of Terrorism*, October 18, 2002, nationalacademies.org.

40. Association of American Universities and other organizations' letter to White House science adviser John Marburger, January 31, 2003, www.aau.edu. See also "Universities Urged to Protect Academic Freedom in Face of War," *Chronicle of Higher Education*, January 31, 2003.

41. National Academies, *Statement on Science and Security in an Age of Terrorism*, October 18, 2002.

42. Ibid.

43. Marburger, remarks to the National Academies of Science Round-

table; and speech at the American Association for the Advancement of Science, Science and Technology Policy Colloquium.

44. AAUP, *Academic Freedom and National Security in a Time of Crisis* (October 2003), n. 1, 43.

45. Knezo, *Possible Impacts of Major Counter Terrorism Security Actions*, n. 1, 18.

46. Ibid., 20.

47. Ibid., 19.

48. Ibid., 25.

49. Ibid., 24.

50. Ibid., 26.

51. MIT, *In the Public Interest*, iii.

52. House Committee, *Conducting Research during the War on Terrorism*, 107th Cong., 2d sess., segment 1, p. 54.

53. Association of American Universities letter, October 15, 2002.

54. "One Year Later: Tighter Security Reshapes Research," *Science*, September 6, 2002; "Universities Urged to Protect Academic Freedom in Face of War."

55. Charles Vest, *Response and Responsibility: Balancing Security and Openness in Research and Education*, Report of MIT President for the Academic Year 2001–2, 8.

56. "Academia Becomes Target for New Security Laws."

57. "University of Texas Medical Branch Cites National Security in Denying Request for Data," *Chronicle of Higher Education*, September 5, 2003.

58. "Restrictions Threaten Science," *Scientist*, December 16, 2002.

59. On this issue see, for example, "World's Most Dangerous Germs: Coming to a Campus Near You?" *Chronicle of Higher Education*, April 25, 2003.

60. National Academies, *Balanced Approach Needed to Mitigate Threats from Bioterrorism without Hindering Progress in Biotechnology*, October 8, 2003; *Biotechnology Research in an Age of Terrorism*, Report of the National Academies, National Research Council (2003).

Chapter 6

1. Among the few comparative studies of antiterrorism policy is Yonah Alexander, ed., *Combating Terrorism: Strategies of Ten Countries* (Ann Arbor: University of Michigan Press, 2002).

2. Quoted in Christopher Michaelsen, "International Human Rights on Trial: The United Kingdom's and Australia's Legal Response to 9/11," *Sydney Law Review* 25 (2003): 275–303 (quote is on p. 276).

3. *U.K. Home Office Summary of Terrorism Legislation*, www.homeoffice

.gov.uk. Summaries are also available on the Liberty web site, www.your-rights.org.uk and www.liberty-human-rights.org.uk (along with all Liberty documents referenced here). The 2000 Terrorism Act and the 2001 Anti-Terrorism Act are available in full text at www.hmso.gov.uk, along with useful explanatory notes for each. For helpful commentaries, see Liberty, *Anti-Terrorism Legislation in the United Kingdom* (2002); John Strawson, ed., *Law after Ground Zero* (London: Cavendish/Glasshouse Press, 2003); Sally Broadbridge, *The Anti-Terrorism, Crime, and Security Bill: Introduction and Summary,* House of Commons Library (November 2001); Kavita Modi and John Wadham, *Anti-Terrorism Legislation in the United Kingdom and the Human Rights Concerns Arising from It* (Liberty, March 2003). For a critical foreign view, see Human Rights Watch (U.S.), *Commentary on the Anti-Terrorism, Crime, and Security Bill 2001* (November 2001), www.hrw.org. For another comparative view, see Philip A. Thomas, "Emergency and Anti-Terrorist Power: 9/11: USA and UK," *Fordham International Law Journal* 26 (2003): 1193–1233.

4. *U.K. Home Office Summary of Terrorism Legislation.*

5. Ibid.

6. Adam Tomkins, "Legislating Against Terror," *Public Law* (summer 2002), 205, quoted in Michaelsen, "International Human Rights on Trial," n. 1.

7. Gareth Pierce, "Internment: The Truth behind the 'War on Terror,'" Liberty Lecture at the London School of Economics, December 15, 2003, www.cacc.org.uk; *Guardian,* July 11, 2003.

8. Pierce, "Internment."

9. John Wadham, "Terror Law Takes Liberties," *Guardian,* March 10, 2002.

10. John Wadham, "Innocents Are Going to Be Locked Up," *Guardian,* November 21, 2001.

11. See Liberty, *Internment of Terrorist Suspects Is Discriminatory, Breaches Human Rights Convention—SIAC Judgment Today,* July 30, 2002; Liberty, *Discriminatory Internment of "Terrorist Suspects": Home Office Wins Appeal,* October 25, 2002.

12. Wadham, "Innocents Are Going to Be Locked Up."

13. Pierce, "Internment."

14. Liberty, Gloucestershire Weapons Inspectors, and Berkshire CIA, *Casualty of War: 8 Weeks of Counter-Terrorism in Rural England* (July 2003) at www.liberty_human_rights.org.uk.

15. "Scrap Anti-Terror Detention Law," British Broadcasting Corporation, December 18, 2003.

16. On the criticism and reaction, see "Blunkett Defiant after Archbishop's Attack on Detention," *Independent,* December 22, 2003.

17. "Watchdog Says Terror Suspects Could Be Deported," *Guardian*, February 12, 2004.

18. Liberty, *Queen's Speech Exposes the "Authoritarianism" at the Heart of the Government*, November 26, 2003.

19. An initial Liberty commentary is *Liberty Response to the Draft Civil Contingency Bill* (August 2003); later is *Liberty's Second Reading Briefing on the Civil Contingencies Bill in the House of Commons* (January 2004).

20. Liberty, *Response to Government's Civil Contingencies Bill*, January 7, 2004.

21. "Government Backs down on Terror Bill," *Guardian*, January 7, 2004; "MPs Welcome Rethink on Anti-Terror Plans," *Guardian*, January 8, 2004.

22. "CPS Chief Resists Blunkett Plan," *Guardian*, February 10, 2004.

23. See, for example, "Blunkett Anti-Terror Proposals Condemned," *Guardian*, February 2, 2004; "In Terror of Blunkett's Security Measures," *Guardian*, February 3, 2004; "Lawyers Attack Blunkett Anti-Terror Plan," *Guardian*, February 7, 2004; as well as numerous articles from other British newspapers.

24. For a range of critical stories, see the Katherine Gun page at the Liberty web site, www.liberty_human_rights.org.uk. On the dismissal of charges, see *Iraq War "Spy Memo Case" Collapses*, CNN, February 25, 2004, www.cnn.com (accessed March 1, 2004).

25. Wadham, "Terror Law Takes Liberties."

26. Michaelsen, "International Human Rights on Trial."

27. "ASIO Spying on the Increase," *Sunday Herald Sun* (Australia), June 29, 2003.

28. Michaelsen, "International Human Rights on Trial."

29. David Kinley and Penny Martin, "International Human Rights Law at Home: Addressing the Politics of Denial," *Melbourne University Law Review* 26 (August 2002): 466–77, quotation at 471.

30. Michaelsen, "International Human Rights on Trial," n. 25, 281. Other useful materials on the Australian situation include Nathan Hancock, *Terrorism and the Law in Australia: Legislation, Commentary, and Constraints* (Research Paper 12, Parliamentary Library, Parliament of Australia, 2001–2); Michael Head, "'Counter-Terrorism' Laws: A Threat to Political Freedom, Civil Liberties, and Constitutional Rights," *Melbourne University Law Review* 26 (December 2002): 666–89.

31. *Liberty Victoria Submission to the Senate Legal and Constitutional Affairs Committee*, April 12, 2002.

32. Chris Maxwell, "September 11 and Its Aftermath: Challenges for Lawyers and the Rule of Law" (address to Maddock Lonie and Chisholm law firm, April 15, 2002), 11.

33. Kinley and Martin, "International Human Rights Law at Home," 199.

34. "ASIO Spying on the Increase," *Sunday Herald Sun*, June 29, 2003.

35. Michaelsen, "International Human Rights on Trial," 281.

36. Ibid. See also Australian Human Rights and Equal Opportunity Commission, *Submission to the Parliamentary Joint Committee on ASIA, ASIS and DSD* (May 23, 2002).

37. Michael Head, "Australian Government Forced to Delay 'Anti-Terrorism' Laws," Australian Civil Liberties Union, May 25, 2002; "Labor Drafts Softer Version of ASIO Detention Powers," *Age* (Melbourne), November 19, 2002; "Another Face-Down over ASIO Bill," *Sunday Age* (Melbourne), February 2, 2003.

38. Australian Human Rights and Equal Opportunity Commission, *Statement on the Australian Security Intelligence Organisation Legislation Amendment (Terrorism) Act* (June 27, 2003).

39. Justice Derrington, "The Terrorist Threat: Australia's Response," *Indiana International and Comparative Law Review* 13 (2003): 699–704.

40. Ibid.

41. Ibid., 702.

42. Justice Michael Kirby, "Australian Law—after 11 September 2001," *Australian Bar Review* 21 (November 5, 2001): 32, 34–35; available at www.hcourt.gov.au/speeches/kirbyj/kirbyj_after11sep01.htm.

43. "The Charges against David Hicks," *Age*, June 14, 2004.

44. "Jews in Australia Were Al-Qaeda Targets, Court Told," *Age*, May 20, 2004; "Canberra Told of Bombing Plot," *Age*, May 18, 2004.

45. "Coalition Reviews Anti-Terror Laws," *Age*, March 29, 2004; "Moves to Alter Law after Terror Suspect Wins Bail," *Age*, June 4, 2004; "Balance of Justice and National Security, or Blindfold for the Courts?" *Age*, June 5, 2004.

46. South Asia Human Rights Documentation Centre, *Prevention of Terrorism Ordinance 2001: Government Decides to Play Judge and Jury* (New Delhi, November 2001); "POTO: Taking the Lawless Road," *Economic and Political Weekly* (Mumbai), December 8, 2001. See also Amnesty International commentary in *New Ordinance Raises Concerns*, AI Index: ASA 20/047/2001 (October 19, 2001); Human Rights Watch, *In the Name of Counter-Terrorism: Human Rights Abuses Worldwide; Country Studies: The Human Rights Impact of Counter-Terrorism Measures in Ten Countries (India)* (March 2003); Smita Narula, "Overlooked Danger: The Security and Rights Implications of Hindu Nationalism in India," *Harvard Human Rights Journal* 16 (2003): 41–68.

47. *POTA Raj in Adivasi Heartland: Misuse of Anti-Terror Law in Jharkhand State of India*, Indigenous Issues, Asian Indigenous and Tribal Peoples Network (New Delhi, February 2003), 3.

48. South Asia Human Rights Documentation Centre, *Prevention of Terrorism Ordinance 2001*, 2.

49. Ibid., 4.

50. Ibid., 2, 3.

51. *POTA Raj in Adivasi Heartland*, 2.

52. On this process, see, for example, Rajeev Dhavan, "POTO and POTA: A Resolution," *Hindu* (New Delhi), December 14, 2001; "From POTO to POTA," *Hindu*, March 28, 2002; "POTA Prospects," *Frontline* (New Delhi), March 30–April 12, 2002.

53. The text of the act is available at www.satp.org.

54. *POTA Raj in Adivasi Heartland*, 6.

55. "POTA Being Used Selectively in Gujarat," *Hindu*, April 27, 2003.

56. *POTA Raj in Adivasi Heartland*, n. 51.

57. *Times of India*, February 20, 2003, cited in *POTA Raj in Adivasi Heartland*.

58. *POTA Raj in Adivasi Heartland*, 7. Other reports on the uses of POTA are "POTA: Freedom to Terrorise," *Economic and Political Weekly*, July 19, 2002; Kuldip Nayar, "Authoritarian Impulses," *Hindu*, July 22, 2002; "POTA: Well-Founded Fears," *Economic and Political Weekly*, April 5, 2003. For useful commentaries, see Rajeev Dhavan, "Misplaced Jingoism," *Hindu*, May 31, 2002; "Justice in a Secular Society," *Hindu*, October 3, 2003. For a foreign view, see India, in *Human Rights Watch World Report 2003*.

59. "POTA Panel Begins Review," *Hindu*, July 9, 2003; "Ordinance to Amend POTA Promulgated," *Hindu*, October 28, 2003.

60. "Jharkhand Leading User of POTA," *Hindu*, June 12, 2004.

61. "POTA Will Be Scrapped before Expiry," *Hindu*, June 12, 2004; "POTA Will Be Repealed: President," *Hindu*, June 8, 2004.

62. "Alternative to POTA: Assembly Passes Bill," *Hindu*, June 3, 2004. On these developments, see Rajeev Dhavan, "Reconstructing India," *Hindu*, May 31, 2004.

Conclusion

1. See Raneta Lawson Mack and Michael J. Kelly, *Equal Justice in the Balance: America's Legal Responses to the Emerging Terrorist Threat* (Ann Arbor: University of Michigan Press, 2004), for an excellent review of these strategies.

2. For one cataloging effort, see www.aclu.org/SafeandFree.

3. On the libertarian community, see "Libertarians Fight Patriot Act," *Newsday*, November 18, 2003; "Odd Bedfellows Fall in Line," *Christian Science Monitor*, October 29, 2003.

4. Interview with ACLU official, July 2004.

5. Ibid.

6. Interview with Anthony Romero, July 2004.

7. Quoted in "On Terror, Spying and Guns, Ashcroft Expands Reach," *New York Times*, March 15, 2002.

8. "Seven Days," *New York Daily News*, December 1, 2002.

9. "By Hiring Barr, ACLU Mixes In a Right With Its Left," *Washington Post*, November 26, 2002; see also "Conservative Favorites to Join ACLU," *USA Today*, November 25, 2002; "Six Weeks in Autumn," *Washington Post*, October 27, 2002; "ACLU Rises on Conservative Tide," *Baltimore Sun*, February 8, 2003.

10. Interview with Anthony Romero, July 2004; interview with ACLU official, July 2004.

11. See, for example, "New Patriot Act Creates Uproar: Uncommon Allies Vowing to Fight Still-Secret Bill," *Seattle Times*, April 15, 2003.

12. "Planned Sequel to Patriot Act Losing Audience," *Los Angeles Times*, July 29, 2003

13. For the focus on the ACLU, see the Justice Department's Patriot Act defense program and particularly Department of Justice, *Dispelling the Myths;* for shoring up efforts, see Attorney General Ashcroft, "Attorney General Ashcroft Speaks about the Patriot Act" (remarks to the American Enterprise Institute, August 19, 2003), both available at www.lifeandliberty.gov.

14. See, for example, "Ashcroft's Agenda," *Baltimore Sun*, February 16, 2003.

15. "The Patriot Act Has Led Online Buyers and Sellers to Watch What They Do: Could It Threaten Internet Business?" *New York Times*, October 13, 2003.

Further Readings

United States

Brill, Stephen. *After: How America Confronted the September 12 Era*. New York: Simon and Schuster, 2003.

Brown, Cynthia, ed. *Lost Liberties: Ashcroft and the Assault on Personal Freedom*. New York: New Press, 2003.

Chang, Nancy. *Silencing Political Dissent: How Post–September 11 Anti-Terrorism Measures Threaten Our Civil Liberties*. New York: Seven Stories Press, 2002.

Cole, David. *Enemy Aliens: Double Standards and Constitutional Freedoms in the War on Terrorism*. New York: New Press, 2003.

Cole, David, and James X. Dempsey. *Terrorism and the Constitution: Sacrificing Civil Liberties in the Name of National Security*. New York: New Press, 2002.

Hentoff, Nat. *The War on the Bill of Rights and the Gathering Resistance*. New York: Seven Stories Press, 2003.

Heynman, Philip. *Terrorism, Freedom, and Security: Winning without War*. Cambridge: MIT Press, 2004.

Leone, Richard C., and Greg Anrig, Jr., eds. *The War on Our Freedoms: Civil Liberties in an Age of Terrorism*. New York: Century Foundation, 2003.

Levy, Barry S., and Victor W. Sidel, eds. *Terrorism and Public Health: A Balanced Approach to Strengthening Systems and Protecting People*. New York: Oxford University Press, 2003.

Mack, Raneta Lawson, and Michael J. Kelly. *Equal Justice in the Balance: America's Legal Responses to the Emerging Terrorist Threat*. Ann Arbor: University of Michigan Press, 2004.

Schulhofer, Stephen J. *The Enemy Within: Intelligence Gathering, Law Enforcement, and Civil Liberties in the Wake of September 11*. New York: Century Foundation, 2002.

Williams, C. Michael. *No Greater Threat: America after September 11 and the Rise of a National Security State*. New York: Algora Publishing, 2002.

Materials published by the American Civil Liberties Union are important critical statements on the situation since September 11. Those publications are accessible at www.aclu.org. In addition to reports and publications, speeches by Anthony Romero, Laura Murphy, Barry Steinhardt, and other senior ACLU staff are particularly useful. See also materials available from the Electronic Privacy Information Center (www.epic.org), Human Rights First (formerly the Lawyers Committee for Human Rights, www.humanrightsfirst.org), Cato Institute (www.cato.org), Human Rights Watch (www.hrw.org), and other organizations.

Human Rights First (Lawyers Committee for Human Rights). *Assessing the New Normal: Liberty and Security for the Post–September 11 United States*. 2003.

Great Britain

Liberty. *Anti-Terrorism Legislation in the United Kingdom*. 2002.

Modi, Kavita, and John Wadham. *Anti-Terrorism Legislation in the United Kingdom and the Human Rights Concerns Arising from It*. Liberty, 2003. March.

Strawson, John, ed. *Law after Ground Zero*. London: Cavendish/Glasshouse Press, 2003.

Australia

Head, Michael. "'Counter-Terrorism' Laws: A Threat to Political Freedom, Civil Liberties, and Constitutional Rights." *Melbourne University Law Review* 26 (December 2002): 666–89.

Kirby, Justice Michael. "Australian Law—after 11 September 2001." *Australian Bar Review* 21 (November 5, 2001): 32, 34–35; available at www.hcourt.gov.au/speeches/kirbyj/kirbyj_after11sep01.htm.

Michaelsen, Christopher. "International Human Rights on Trial: The United Kingdom's and Australia's Legal Response to 9/11." *Sydney Law Review* 25 (2003): 275–303.

India

Human Rights Watch. *In the Name of Counter-Terrorism: Human Rights Abuses Worldwide; Country Studies: The Human Rights Impact of Counter-Terrorism Measures in Ten Countries (India)*. 2003. March.

POTA Raj in Adivasi Heartland: Misuse of Anti-Terror Law in Jharkhand State of India. Indigenous Issues, Asian Indigenous and Tribal Peoples Network. New Delhi, 2003. February.

South Asia Human Rights Documentation Centre. *Prevention of Terrorism Ordinance 2001: Government Decides to Play Judge and Jury.* New Delhi, 2001. November.

Index

211